BETTERING AMERICAN POETRY
2015

BETTERING AMERICAN POETRY 2015

AN ANTHOLOGY

EDITORS:
Kenzie Allen
Eunsong Kim
Amy King
Jason Koo
Héctor Ramírez
Metta Sáma
Vanessa Angelica Villarreal
Nikki Wallschlaeger

CONTRIBUTING EDITORS:
Sarah Clark
Airea D. Matthews

Bettering Books
New York, NY

BETTERING AMERICAN POETRY 2015
Copyright © 2017

Published by Bettering Books

Cover Art & Design by Dia Lacina © 2016

First Edition
ISBN: 978-0692830901
Library of Congress Control Number: 2017900693

Bettering Books
New York, NY

BetterAmericanPoetry@gmail.com

Table of Contents

Introduction

We are writing this introduction to an anthology of poetry from 2015 in 2016, with 2017 only a few months away. As we write this, the poems in this anthology are already a year old. As you read this, who knows how old they've grown. This book is the result of editors contributing their labor as an act of love, justice, and care for their communities. So while this book may be a bit late, any project borne of unpaid labor and limited access to time and resources will suffer delays, exhaustion, and debate according to a difference in ideals.

But it's finally here.

It happened like this: in September 2015, David Lehman, series editor of *Best American Poetry*, failed to publicly address or even acknowledge that a Midwestern cis white man, Michael Derrick Hudson, openly admitted to using an Asian-American *nom de plume* to increase the chances of his poem's publication. To Hudson, writers of color and women have an easier time getting published by virtue of their "ethnic-sounding" surnames, the underlying assumption being that men with white-sounding names were at a *disadvantage* in the publishing world.

Hudson's poem was not a product of lived Asian, femme experience. The dissonance between the name and the poem is eerie and violent. A white man had forced his words into an Asian woman's mouth.

The tactic was nothing short of a neocolonial charade, a brazen invocation of yellowface minstrelsy for the sake of boosting the literary publications of one white man. And the poem produced by such a maneuver was honored as one of the Best of 2015.

This, in and of itself, is a major offense to say the least. To add insult to injury, Lehman and Hudson remained silent, and guest editor Sherman Alexie had to shoulder the public responsibility and take the fall for this debacle. Adding further insult to that injury, Alexie, in a defense of his decision, introduced readers to the term "racial nepotism," which delighted those in favor of the literary status quo and dismayed those who resist it, particularly dissenting poets of color. Establishment poets and critics were quick to flaunt their allegiance to Alexie and deploy his coinage against those poets and writers of color who critiqued the decision to publish and celebrate Hudson's poem, accusing them of adhering to this double standard of so-called racial nepotism.

And so this is what our critique was reduced to. According to the defenders of BAP and the gatekeepers of American poetry as such, doing one's best to examine axes of oppression and amplify the voices of the unheard through direct action essentially replicates the position of, say, the Ivy League dynasty white boy who has a six figure gig waiting for him after graduation thanks to daddy's handshakes and donations—same move, they argued, but different context.

And all the while, the women, the POC, and the LGBTQIA+ voices in that anthology, rightfully thrilled to see their hard work and excellent poetry celebrated by those with poetical clout, were eclipsed by a white man whose sense of entitlement took center stage until the scandal ran its course.

It was 2015 and we, the ten editors of this anthology, were angry at what we were seeing and hearing. More than angry, we were enraged. Exhausted. Fired up. And not because 2015 was somehow special. Not because 2015 was a singular year for various forms of violence targeting communities of difference—no, we know well that such violence is largely the story of America itself since its conception. And each of us had been feeling enraged, exhausted, fired up, and more for countless different reasons and for many different spans of time. Nevertheless, 2015 brought us together on this project, and we were eager to begin.

Because we were sick of literary gatekeepers laying claim to the word "best."

We were done with publications that pretended to a radical poetics with little more than a fig leaf of diversity to cover its white supremacist foundations.

We were disgusted by all-white, all-male University syllabi that pretended to teach young writers the names of the writers they needed to know if they wanted to get anywhere in the literary world.

We felt defeated and emotionally drained by the majority white male tenured professors who crafted and defended such syllabi.

We were exhausted from the out-of-body experience of having to watch our own tokenizations from the sidelines of our literary ambitions.

We were too aware of the abuses that occur in ostensible safe spaces in the literary world, heartbroken for those among us who fell victim to violence, exclusion, and erasure at the hands of members of their own alleged communities.

We had too many of our brilliant fellow poets confide in us that they were ready to exit the poetry world for good.

We were fed up with seeing a poem's worth measured only by the weight of its author's previous publications, standing in academia, or proximity to the poetry elite.

We still are. And in 2015 we felt ready to respond, so we put out a call for nominations of poems.

Which isn't to say that any of us were agreeing on anything like an aesthetic, or an approach, or a tactic when Amy King had the idea to start this project. We hardly agreed on the name, *Bettering American Poetry,* and we likely still don't. We are, after all, ten distinct readers, writers, and lovers of poetry, with ten different complexes of ideas about what exactly needs to be done in order to achieve real change in our too-often violent, too-often self-serving, and too-often power-driven poetry world.

Still, our differences didn't prevent us from doing the work then, and don't now. On the contrary, we are proud of the variegated and multi-textured anthology we have been able to piece together precisely because our ten different approaches. And really, all that mattered for the nascence of this work was that in 2015 each of us shared ten different parts of the same rage.

When we set out to make this anthology happen, we knew that the old models of collecting and sharing contemporary poetry were obviously inadequate. Anonymous submissions and token guest editors and pretense toward collecting only the "best" would not achieve any kind of parity in the literary world. We knew this. We hadn't come close to parity yet, and the old ways of doing things showed no real signs of ever getting us there anytime soon. We needed more disruption. Because in September 2015, perhaps the most important thing that we co-editors agreed upon was that the poetry world was for the most part still operating under the same metrics of cisgender, straight, male, capitalist white supremacist tastes that had produced entitled white poets like Hudson and protected institutions like BAP in the first place. The gatekeepers told us what was the best, but what we needed was something else.

So if those gatekeepers and tastemakers of American poetics called us racial nepotists when we loudly critiqued Hudson and Lehman, we decided to do nothing to actively avoid that label. Our call for poems was as widespread and open as possible, but we did not limit ourselves from directly soliciting the poets we admired. Many of these poets we knew personally, or knew through Twitter, or met at some conference one time. Many were total strangers. We didn't care. Pretending to any kind of objective, utopic, level-playing-field, anonymous, or scientific approach to separating the wheat from the chaff was never our aim nor has it ever been honestly possible in our line of work. We the co-editors of this anthology are incapable of objectifying our taste, nor do we believe that any editor is so capable—such a premise, in the end, merely preserves privilege and reifies the literary status quo. When we write our own poems, we are constantly aware of the dominant poetics inscribed into our skin, we are too alert to the languages that we are supposed to replicate on the page, and we actively resist our programming as much as we can every day. How can we pretend to do any differently when selecting poems for an anthology like this one?

So we committed ourselves to the radical act of centering marginalized poets, selecting the work that thoroughly-challenged and uplifted us, and forging a list of poets that in and of itself was a defiant statement against the dominant and oppressive American poetics we live and work under. And to the best of our abilities, we did not allow our personal lives or our personal tastes prevent us from doing this work.

Each editor had their own unique approach for making their selections for this anthology, whether that meant deliberately seeking out nominated poets that they never heard of or soliciting the work of a poet they had already long admired. And for the record, if it wasn't clear enough already, we do not consider this latter act tantamount to any form of nepotism, racial or otherwise. Nepotism is the politics of getting further ahead; we are interested in the poetics of self-defense. This anthology is a move toward the anti-objective empowerment and amplification of voices that, by their existence alone, resist the obliterating power of the

American State and status quo—the kind of voices that kept us alive in 2015. Each editor simply made the decisions that they felt would move us in that direction.

Again, we are ten different editors with ten different reasons for joining a project like this one. But what we do share as of this anthology's publication is a deep sense of awe and gratitude. Each of us is staggered by the brilliance and courage of the very different writers in this collection, and we are honored to have brought them together between the covers of the same book. And we hope that perhaps this anthology can serve as one of many blueprints for more such work in the coming years.

The work we began in 2015 took time. And as 2015 became 2016, we saw more of the same American violence appear in different costumes. Another poetry scandal. Another microaggression at work or in a grad school workshop. Another hypermasculine Hollywood whitewash. Another cultural appropriation in pop music. And, meanwhile and always: more state-sanctioned murder. More protests. More cultural and environmental destruction. More depression, more rage. Another farcical and terrifying campaign season. More poetry, and still more loss.

And now as 2016 becomes 2017, it may already seem unintuitive and counterproductive to look back at 2015. After all, there is far too much work to be done, and it needs to be done now. It needed to be done yesterday. There is no time to waste. And so, some might wonder what use 2015 is to us immediately, here and now as 2016 becomes 2017 and a Trump presidency is a legitimate possibility and every day between now and November means more structural pain.

But one thing that 2015 taught us, or rather reminded us, is this: each and every one of us must exercise our memories daily. We are all living in a time of violence that inundates, politics that obliterate, and the kind of rhetoric that numbs us to the sense of being alive and awake. Many of us feel constantly depleted just trying to keep up with the blistering pace of the violence that bombards the most marginalized among us—and we still feel as though our heads are barely above the water. This is to say nothing of the additional work required, beyond the point of exhaustion, to take any kind of step toward effecting structural change. And yet, somewhere in all this exhausting labor we must also carve out spaces in time to allow ourselves to pause, to remember. It is our duty to remember the names of the dead. The faces of the disappeared. The lessons of our ancestors. And poetry grants us these moments of pause. Hopefully, this anthology will become another radical act of pause, or in the very least will increase our appetites for remembering.

None of what we are doing or saying is new. We know this. And anthologies like this one have been made before. But they must continue to be made and made again. And even though the "new" and the "best" may be flashier, sexier, and more marketable ways to anthologize poetry, what we hope to offer with this collection is: the remembered. Because it is so easy now for us to become desensitized to violence. Because it is tempting to keep moving in whatever direction our noses tell us is forward. Because it is as difficult as it is necessary to collectively pause and relive pain alongside one another. Because without meditation and reflection, we relegate the most vulnerable among us to oblivion.

Finally, in the face of such oblivion and to borrow a note from Ross Gay's breathtaking "Catalog of Unabashed Gratitude," we the co-editors of this anthology want to say: thank you.

Thank you to the poets sharing a space in this anthology—we needed you in 2015 and we need you now. We cannot express our gratitude for you fully.

Thank you to the countless other voices who also kept us going but are not named here, this time. Fortunately for us there are too many of you to even begin to name, and all we can say now is that we hope you somehow feel our gratitude every time we share your work, talk you up to a friend, or check out a reading you're giving.

Thank you to the writers who hold down several jobs (paid or not) in order to survive, and/or are parents or caregivers to others, and/or navigate illness and disability (visible or not) on a daily basis yet still somehow make the time to heal and challenge through their words: we recognize that your labor can't ever be quantified, and we thank you again and again for doing it anyway.

Thank you to the poets who have dedicated themselves to building healthier poetry communities, and who courageously defied the ones that proved to be in service of the violent status quo. We hope you are feeling more supported, safe, and loved now than ever before, and if you don't know us by now we hope that it's only a matter of time before our paths cross.

Thank you to the poets, activists, teachers, students, and other role models who betray Whiteness, Heteronormativity, Ableism, Imperial Capitalism, Nationalism(s), and the nexus of powers that continue to preserve our oppressive American way of life. We know as well as you do that America was never Great, and that the work of bettering what we have inherited must be constant if we hope to leave future generations with anything we can call good.

Thank you to the poets who exist in various states of perpetual translation, who must navigate bordered realities and each day pass through checkpoints of documentation, immigration, language/accent, and other state-enforced categorizations that define "American" status—our middle fingers are up to anyone who attempts to contain you, detain you, remove you, or demand that you prove yourself in any way, and we dedicate ourselves to supporting your resilient selves any way you need us to.

Thank you to the poets who risked jobs, friendships, family ties, and senses of self simply by challenging themselves to speak truth to power—thank you for your fortitude, thank you for pressing on, and for every bridge you burn, may a sturdier, healthier one take its place.

And to the poets who suffered in 2015 or are suffering now, whenever now is: we send you our love, we are unspeakably grateful for your existence, and we hope this book can help you heal in some way.

Sincerely,

Héctor Ramírez, Vanessa Angelica Villarreal, Sarah Clark, and Amy King

Dearest Readers,

Southern writers of color live with racialized histories standing as signposts—often literally—everyday, from confederate statues to confederate flags, highway renamings to school namings, airport renamings to park namings, from Civil War markers to Civil War relics, the racialized past is ever present. The question of who is American—thus who is worth protecting—is ever present.

Bettering American Poetry comes at a time where poets once again speak to the political world. It arrives at the very start of this 21st century in which transgender persons are being murdered and assaulted in high numbers. This anthology arrives at a time in which police brutality against citizens, most notably against citizens of color, including the unconscionable murders of children of color, none of whom have been vindicated, is at its most visible. This anthology arrives at a time in which rapists are still protected; one in which women writers are told not to drink at readings in order to avoid potentially being assaulted by male participants. This anthology marks a time in which poets have once again said *enough*, poets who have found, as Audre Lorde said in 1981, a use for their anger.

Reader: I arrive to you in anger frustration despair joy hope, in a belief of not only "bettering" poetry by being constant advocates and activists but that in "bettering" poetry we learn to "better" ourselves to "better" our attitudes to "better" our belief systems to "better" our spirits to "better" our actions.

~M

*
**

Dear Readers,

We can still be better. After the public outcry over Michael Derrick Hudson's yellowfaced inclusion in the *Best American Poetry 2015*, after so many poets, both POC and otherwise, spoke out in rage and/or sympathized via social media, things have predictably gone back to normal, with the *Best American Poetry 2016* appearing as if nothing had ever happened, including poets of color I admire who didn't refuse admission into this bastion of bestness in solidarity with their POC peers—perhaps because their presence there might still mean more than their willed exclusion? Because refusing acceptance into the anthology would allow the likes of Michael Derrick Hudson to have voice over #ActualAsianPoets? Or because the poets had never been admitted and admission into this "best" anthology carries so much weight, professionally and emotionally? Or because they weren't thinking? Or didn't care? What has changed? What can change? I don't know. I have never been included in the *Best*

American Poetry anthology. And because of that many of you will assume that I am not "best" enough to be included. Even after the inclusion of Yi-Fen Chou has made that assumption ludicrous. I am an actual Asian poet with two books to my name—a name which most of you don't know, including many of you Asian American poets. The name Yi-Fen Chou is more well-known than my own. Do you know how this feels, America? You might not hear the *fuck you* in Hudson's "After a poem of mine has been rejected a multitude of times under my real name, I put Yi-Fen's name on it and send it out again. As a strategy for 'placing' poems this has been quite successful for me." But I hear it loud and clear. Sherman Alexie, do you know who I am? David Lehman, do you know who I am? Michael Derrick Hudson, do you know who I am? I can't help but see your names, but you can't help me see mine. I, unfortunately, have to help me see mine. I, and others like me, the other editors of this anthology—those fighting for representational power against power, the power of including other names, other bodies of work, other bodies. Inclusion and representation are not honors bestowed on us for simple bestness, dear readers, but outcomes in an ongoing American civil war. There are people behind these lines. The anthology you hold in your hands is one of the battlegrounds.

—Jason Koo

✻
✻✻

Dear Reader,

Anthologies like the one you are holding in your hands usually stress their timeliness above all else. They tend to pride themselves on their newness, often betraying an urgent desire to be "first" and collect the "best of" that supersedes any commitment to championing vital work from voices of difference. But as a reader and writer, I am as uninterested in the notion of "best" as I am in that of "newest," because neither of these qualifications have ever offered me anything more than added pressure and capitalist anxiety. And I know that I am not alone in feeling this way.

After the other editors and I selected these poems in 2015, time and life and death marched on, and suddenly it was 2017—the dawn of the Trump era, and of the rhetoric of hate and "greatness." But what might seem like a tardiness to some strikes me to be perfectly fitting for the work we've collected: the poets in this anthology are, in their own ways, very familiar with different conceptions of time, and each of the poems here somehow anticipated our current moment. By their empathy, prescience, and positionality, these poems are as much 2017 as they are 2015 (and long before). And more importantly, the poems in this anthology remind us that no span of time can defined by any one man or one event.

There's never been much sense for writers like us to try and play catch-up with the dominant flow of time, because we are in our own ways out-of-step with straight, white, cis, male, wealthy, able-bodied America. We are stuck in the past, wrapped up in futurity. Time, for us, is something to navigate actively; it is a heaviness that we can't easily pass. So, in more ways than one, *Bettering American Poetry 2015* couldn't be a more timely anthology, and I would encourage you, reader, to have time in mind while you approach these poems.

In my family, we'd say a book like this one was published on Mexican time. But each of the poets here has their own sense of time. And all of these temporalities have all been brought together, in this book, for you. I hope you enjoy these poems, from out of time and of their time.

-Héctor Ramírez, 1.1.2017

BETTERING AMERICAN POETRY
2015

Hanif Willis-Abdurraqib

I Don't Remember The Whole Summer When "Do The Right Thing" Dropped

but I do remember the night that police got a hold of Big Mike from North Linden & beat his face into the sweltering brick outside what used to be a Pizza Hut until it got robbed by some southside stick up kids two summers earlier & then my big brother said it had to shut down cuz niggas ain't gonna get a gun held to they head for minimum wage & Mike used to deliver pizzas to the hood before the hood woke up in winter with new hungers & come spring, Mike was rockin' a gold rope 'round his neck thicker than the coils in a hangman's knot & that's when the cops on the eastside began to lick their lips & when their hands started to tremble while whispering 'bout what they would do to him if they ever caught his ass, which maybe explains the way his bright blood painted the abandoned brick & the five police still pressing their heels into his face even after his right eye swung free from its socket, a grisly pendulum & my big brother left me home alone & hungry that night when the whole hood ran from their homes and set upon the police with any weapon they could find & they say that Mike's face was a bloody & wet mess & they say he wasn't breathing or they say he ain't have a mouth anymore or they say all of him was a dark & gaping hole & earlier that day, my big brother hid his white jordans in his bookbag when he came back to the hood from his suburban job & he walked in the door & said we all one handful of gold away from a closed casket funeral & I don't know how many mothers walked from the mouth of that summer childless but I could see the old Pizza Hut burning from my window & I could see a cop being dragged into the bushes by the stickup kids & isn't it funny how art most imitates life when a black body is being drained of it? how easily we can imitate that which is never coming back again to claim its space? & when my big brother came home that night, he carried me to bed with a glass of warm milk & when a drop of blood fell from his knuckles & blended into the white of the glass, I did not ask who it belonged to.

Originally published in *The Offing*.

Hanif Willis-Abdurraqib is a poet and essayist from Columbus, Ohio. His first full-length collection of poems, *The Crown Ain't Worth Much*, was released by Button Poetry in 2016.

The House That Swallows Tears

Bearded gust. Frozen ash. House of looms. House saying, the world disappears when you look at it too long. World without glimmer. The face becomes a butterfly net. Wounded razor. Boiling mirror. Love has a face like a chickenwire fence. Forgotten shelter. Fuss to make time. Change shape to dirge. White dress and clutter. The face balls into a fist. The house snickers like fire. The dead grass says fear is the most divine emotion. The skin of the house rustles. Dust hiding in the light. The house that swallows tears. We are here to burn you down. History is baby's breath and we are hyacinths. People are homesick for fantasies. People are living like drums, beaten by another and in fear of unknown gods. People are being reborn as squalls. People lock themselves away in their bodies and long to escape their braided hair like butterflies. People are breathless and sugar-eyed. People are empty bottles inside of insects. The air thick with the lit house now. The flame unfurls like a year. You are a firefly now, house. It all makes sense in the words of my dead language. The universe gives birth to itself. No-one is able to chop off both hands and toss them in the river without another person's help.

Originally published in *LEFT* .

manuel arturo abreu, born in Santo Domingo, is a poet and artist from the Bronx. Currently based in Portland, they work in text, ephemeral sculpture, and photography. They are the managing editor at Civil Coping Mechanisms, as well as co-founder of home school, a free pop up art school in Portland, OR. Find manuel at twigtech.tumblr.

Aleph Altman-Mills

Letter to My Mouth

Dear autistic mouth,
with your tidepool drool and your keyhole stutter,
I disowned you.
Turned you to mail slot.

You make it so hard to mean what I say
when I hardly know what I'm saying.
I might as well be the Big Bad Wolf
with a tongue full of brick.

Dear manic mouth,
with your bench slat clatter and your leaf blizzard fall,
I disowned you.

You are a hole
in a rubber balloon. Better for pills
than for teeth.

Dear echolalic mouth,
with your skip rope of inside out songs,
I disowned you.
Swallowed reflected light,
broke the mirrors, hid the spoons.

Dear mouth,
you hold so much air, all of me goes balloon dog.
Dear mouth, you hold so much stutter,
all of me goes highway rail. Dear mouth, you are Russian roulette
of gumballed words and stuck elevators. You thank everything
too many times.

Dear broken mouth,
I disowned you.

Take me back.

Originally published in *Words Dance.*

Aleph Altman-Mills is an autistic writer who has been published in *The Legendary, Words Dance*, and *Mobius*, among others. Aleph blogs and posts poetry snippets at really-fucking-confused.tumblr.com.

Pluto Shits on the Universe

On February 7, 1979, Pluto crossed over Neptune's orbit and became the eighth planet from the sun for twenty years. Labeled as "chaotic," Pluto was later discredited from planet status.

Today, I broke your solar system. Oops.
My bad. Your graph said I was supposed
to make a nice little loop around the sun.

Naw.

I chaos like a motherfucker. Ain't no one can chart me.
All the other planets, they think I'm annoying.
They think I'm an escaped moon, running free.

Fuck your moon. Fuck your solar system. Fuck your time.
Your year? Your year ain't shit but a day to me.
I could spend your whole year turning the winds
in my bed. Thinking about rings and how Jupiter
should just pussy on up and marry me by now.

Your day? That's an asswipe. A sniffle.
Your whole day is barely the start of my sunset.

My name means hell, bitch. I am hell, bitch. All the cold
you have yet to feel. Chaos like a motherfucker.
And you tried to order me. Called me ninth.
Somewhere in the mess of graphs and math and compass
you tried to make me follow rules. Rules? Fuck your
rules. Neptune, that bitch slow. And I deserve all the sun
I can get, and all the blue-gold sky I want around me.

It is February 7th, 1979 and my skin is more
copper than any sky will ever be. More metal.
Neptune is bitch-sobbing in my rearview,
and I got my running shoes on and all this sky that's all mine.

Fuck your order. Fuck your time. I realigned the cosmos.
I chaosed all the hell you have yet to feel. Now all your kids
in the classrooms, they confused. All their maps:

wrong. They don't even know what the fuck to do.
They gotta memorize new songs and shit. And the other
planets, I fucked their orbits. I shook the sky. Chaos
like a motherfucker.

Today, I broke your solar system. Oops. My bad.

Originally published in *Poetry* and *The Breakbeat Poets Anthology* (Haymarket Books, 2015).

Fatimah Asghar is a nationally
touring poet, photographer, and
performer. She created Bosnia and
Herzegovina's first spoken word
poetry group, REFLEKS, while on a
Fulbright studying theater in post-
violent contexts. Her work has
appeared or is forthcoming in *Poetry,
PEN Poetry Series, The Paris-
American, The Margins,* and *Gulf
Coast.* She is a Kundiman Fellow and
a member of the Dark Noise
Collective. Her chapbook *After* is
available from YesYes Books.

Amber Atiya

moon above 11433

u daughter of geechee gods
u femme no longer loving
the butch on top of her, u queer
my nickel plated heaven:
boys with breasts
& moustache
girls with hips
& apple
u biceps/white tee turban
round the head & it
don't stop
u condom wrapper beautify
the weeds beautify
the turf wars
u eskovitch this hood
spiked with open cellars
vulgar prose
a zillion mouths chirp
their synchronized hunger
from trees & project windows
u drown police
sirens in soca
u deflower night red
black & green this borough
u illume my low-
end synthetic wig
my boos think u pure
myth
a seahorse, tragic
dragon carved from wet bone
but u pearl-shine
bright/brighter
than any face at land-
lord tenant court

Originally published as part of the PEN Poetry Series, May 2015.

Amber Atiya is a poet, performer, and self-taught book artist-in-training. Her work has appeared in *Boston Review, Nepantla: A Journal Dedicated to Queer Poets of Color*, and on Poetry Foundation's radio and podcast series *PoetryNow*. Amber's chapbook, *the fierce bums of doo-wop*, was chosen for *The Volta*'s Best Books of 2014. She resides in Jamaica, Queens (by way of Brooklyn) and is a member of a women's writing group celebrating 14 years, and counting.

Malaka Badr *translated by Robin Moger*

Pleasant thoughts for getting rid of rage

I have rage enough to burn the city
and murder its inhabitants
individually, each a different way,
with blithe delight unspoiled by guilt.
Rage enough
to make me wish harm even
on bothersome kids,
the elderly, the living dead,
and the embittered, determined to preach their message.
Rage enough
to rip paving stones from the sidewalks
and kick cats in their bellies
and pop the spots on my neighbour's face
and smash the streetlamps,
the ones that never light up when you need them.
Rage enough to enjoy
devising new and twisted ways to kill,
to key cars' paintwork till they bleed
and their alarms plead with me to stop,
to scatter the papers on my boss's desk,
pour the steaming cup of coffee onto colleagues' heads,
aim stones at the cameras mounted
over the heads of us all.
I've rage enough
to turn the cruellest insults on the world,
tell each and every one of them just what they're like,
break off my relationship with the boy,
and nail friends' bodies to the doors
of Downtown's historic buildings,
sipping my coffee by the clotting gore.

I have rage enough to destroy the world entire
and all the cowardice I need to not kill myself first.

Originally published in *qisasukhra.*

Malaka Badr is a poet, journalist, and a translator based in Cairo, Egypt. She published her first book in 2011, a collection of poems entitled *Without Heavy Losses*. Her poems have also appeared in *The Tahrir of Poems*, an anthology of seven contemporary poets from Egypt, published in 2014. She has contributed to a book documenting the Egyptian revolution, on 25th of January 2011, titled *The Diaries of Rage*.

Robin Moger is a professional Arabic to English translator with an interest in contemporary Egyptian writing. He has translated a number of modern Arabic novels, most recently Youssef Rakha's *The Crocodiles* (Seven Stories Press, 2014). His translation of for *Writing Revolution: Voices from Tunis to Damascus* (I.B. Tauris, 2013) won the English PEN award for outstanding writing in translation. Alongside his published translations of poetry and prose, he also posts occasional translations of unpublished literature and essays at qisasukhra.wordpress.com. A former resident of Cairo, Robin now lives in Cape Town.

My Dad Asks "How Come Black Folks Can't Just Write About Flowers"

bijan been dead 11 months & my blue margin reduced to arterial. there's a party at my house, a house held by legislation vocabulary & trill. but hell, it's ours & it sparkle on the corner of view park, a channel of blk electric. danny wants to walk to the ledge up the block, & we an open river of flex: we know what time it is. on the ledge, folk give up neck & dismantle grey navigation for some slice of body. it's june. it's what we do.

walk down the middle of our road, & given view park, a lining of dubois' 10th, a jack n jill feast, & good blk area, it be our road. we own it. I'm sayin' with money. our milk neighbors, collaborate in the happy task of surveillance. they new. they pivot function. they call the khaki uniforms. i swift. review the architecture of desire spun clean, & I could see how we all look like ghosts.

3 squad cars roll up at my door & it's a fucking joke cuz exactly no squad cars rolled up to the mcdonald's bijan was shot at & exactly no squad cars rolled up to find the murders & exactly no one did what could be categorized as they "job," depending on how you define time spent for money earned for property & it didn't make me feel like I could see less of the gun in her holster because she was blk & short & a woman, too. she go,

"this your house?"
I say, "yea." she go,
"can you prove it?"
I say, "it mine."
she go, "ID?" I say, "it mine."
she go, "backup," on the sly
& interview me, going all, "what's your address— don't look!"
& hugh say, "I feel wild disrespected."

& white go, "can you explain that?"

& danny say, "how far the nearest precinct?"

& christian say, "fuck that."

& white go, "can you explain that?"

I cross my arms. I'm bored & headlights quit being interesting after I called 911 when I was 2 years old because it was the only phone number I knew by heart.

Originally published in *Winter Tangerine.*

Aziza Barnes is blk & alive. Born in Los Angeles, Aziza currently lives in Oxford, Mississippi. Their first chapbook*, me Aunt Jemima and the nailgun,* was the first winner of the Exploding Pinecone Prize and published from Button Poetry. Winner of the 2015 Pamet River Prize Aziza's first full length collection *i be but i ain't,* is from YesYes Books in 2016.

Blackbody Curve

Stairs: a rushed flight down thirty-eight; French doors unlocked always.

Always: a lie; an argument.

Argument: two buck hunters circle a meadow's edge.

Edge: one of us outside bleeding.

Bleeding: shards of glass; doors locked.

Locked: carpet awash with blood.

Blood: lift and drop; a sudden breeze.

Breeze: its whistle though bone.

Bone: the other was looking at —

Bone: cradle to catch drips.

Drips: quiet as a meadow fawn.

Fawn: faces down each hunter each gun.

Gun: again.

Again: somebody call someone.

Someone: almost always prefers forgetting.

Forgetting: an argument; a lie.

Lie: a meadow; a casement; a stair.

Originally published in *Poetry*.

Ha ha ha niggers are the worst

you know like how she would lie down in her dark cornered room with an old movie and remember again just how normal just everyday just cold just buck wild casual just sidewalk crack each smack in the face was just every day buried in every part of speech just life and she was just all in it you too you'd just go ha ha ha niggers are the worst remember and not even stop to think about why her stomach hurt how come she had all that pain in her side or the side of her head why she needs new glasses just ha ha ha niggers are the worst and sometimes she stood big as a house and sometimes she was a house and the neighbors wished she'd keep her blinds closed please wished she'd pick up and move please but there's so much to lift so much to move   what she's not allowed to say i'm lonely   what she's not allowed to say   this is hard   what she's not allowed to say   i wish someone would hold me would let me hold them for just one full minute   what she's not   allowed to do   cry where we can see her   and laugh   ha ha ha   ha ha ha   ha ha ha niggers are the worst   remember?   ha ha ha   ha ha ha   ha ha ha ha ha ha nig-

Originally published in *Nepantla: A Journal Dedicated to Queer Poets of Color.*

Samiya Bashir's books of poetry, *Field Theories* (forthcoming), *Gospel,* and *Where the Apple Falls,* and anthologies, including *Role Call: A Generational Anthology of Social & Political Black Literature & Art,* exist. Sometimes she makes poems of dirt. Sometimes zeros and ones. Sometimes variously rendered text. Sometimes light. She lives in Portland, Ore, with a magic cat who shares her obsessions with trees and blackbirds and occasionally crashes her classes and poetry salons at Reed College.

Jenny Boully

The satchel empty by the time the fall falls around

The satchel empty by the time the fall
falls around: That was the point of it
all to have the empty. Once there was
a snowfall and that had been an adven-
ture but the teachers wouldn't let
us go outside to feel it. I had wanted
very badly to feel it. By the time
our mother showed up to get us my sis-
ter and me there was hardly any-
thing left a little snowbird—or so
it seemed—stuffed into a crook of
a tree. The letters they tried
to teach me I could only
learn if they were pretty. There had been
some letters that were pretty. The G was
glittery grape easily traced. I had tried to learn
and be good but the teachers did not
like me and the boys had wanted to harm
me and so that is why I said that the cake was baked
before the ingredients were even mixed so I could escape
recess. It has been so long now since I was punished
for having drawn the poodle dog before anyone even
told me. The world is waving and fluctu-
ates. There was a cost I am now learning. There
had been a consequence and then there was-
n't. There was more to bear. My daughter—
I have grown I realize so old—presses
her face to the glass. When I'm that close
she says it's purple outside.

Originally published in *Dusie.*

Jenny Boully is the author of *The Body: An Essay, The Book of Beginnings and Endings: Essays, not merely because of the unknown that was stalking toward them,* and other books.

Essay on Synonyms for Tender and a Confession
for Sandra Maria Esteves

Color it all blue:

        my father and my father's father and his. *Marcelo, Marcelo, Marcelo.*

And all of us in one suitcase that hasn't been opened.
I haven't been opened.

        I want to be all pink. For one day;
to name each part of me after the names of my mother's lovers,
to throw my head back and dance like someone pretty,
        or just hold the shame in my hand.

My name a two hundred year old word for *Please.*

        As in, please let me open the suitcase.
        As in, please let me play whatever is inside.

And sometimes my name talks to me.
        It says, you ain't shit.

        It says even the priests are lonely.
It comes to me as one priest confessing to another:

Marcelo, I want the red dress
and to throw my hair up real beauty queen style.

        Marcelo, I wanted a gun.
        I'm not ready to be dipped in water.

Like you, like a father.

         And so I opened the lid
     and held each flute inside like shattered glass

because I know that my father's name is my name
       and because I know he can hurt me still,

                 as he does himself,
           thinking he's doing it to himself,

    thinking there's no difference,
    which there isn't.

But there was no song, there was hardly any glitter.

    No twins to be had.

And the priest who is no longer Marcelo,
       and the flute who is no longer Marcelo.

    I don't know what it means to name a child.
    When he said my name, I opened his eyes.

       I played the song.

       Neither of us knew how it ended.
We would have paid anything at all to make it stop.

Originally published in *Poem-a-Day*.

Marcelo Hernandez Castillo is a Canto Mundo fellow and the first undocumented student to graduate from the University of Michigan's MFA program. He teaches summers as the resident artist at the Atlantic Center for the Arts in Florida. He was a finalist for the *New England Review* Emerging Writer Award and his manuscript was a finalist for the Alice James Book Prize and the National Poetry Series. His poems and essays can be found in *Indiana Review, New England Review, The Paris American, Gulf Coast,* and *Southern Humanities Review,* among others. He helped initiate the Undocupoets campaign which successfully eliminated citizenship requirements from all major first poetry book prizes in the country.

Chopped: Four Sections

X

Reading the Yelp reviews of your family's restaurant—you have made a mistake. *"Lacking any lasting impression." "The food is good, but the service is awful." "Waitstaff is surly and inattentive."* Twenty-three reviews. Your mother's English, bandaged with smiles, your father's eyes peeking out from the kitchen, and your brother, who remains an asshole in every description. Lauren M. details in a one-star review an argument over a delivery that he brought to her house. It is so authentic—it is painful to read. Your brother becomes angry and slams a full box of food onto her driveway. In February, the steam rises from the wet noodles on the asphalt, rising with his heavy breathing. Your brother is thirty-two and has spent exactly half his life working there. Your mother has shingles and no doctor. Your father has hypertension and no doctor. You have a college degree and will not go back there. Lauren M.'s profile has zero friends and one review.

X

Yesterday, you took a shit so big at the office that it refused to flush. It was a Monday. You remember your old roommate once said that food is like paying rent to your body. In which case, do you have a roommate? How can you afford it? How do you live like this? When you yanked the lever to draw another surge of water, the shit stayed—dense and staid, once, twice, three, four, five times—unimpressed by the rush of plumbing. The clear and swirling water around a single object. So terrified of your own feces, it's patriotic, you stare into the bowl with great reverential anxiety. It is like history: private—that only the parts of you unseen have memory of its creation, while your mind's faculty flees. What in this world is so defiant, so honest and immune to eviction, that it dares you to destroy it with your own bare hands?

X

After the intake therapist rejects your bid at an Adderall prescription, she informs you that you have a learning disorder. Also, it seems you have been bordering on depression for a while now. She looks so serious. How long have you been like this? How do you live—like this? You reject your first therapist when you meet her, an Asian woman who unsettles you by her likeness and academic English. As you backpedal from her office you feel yourself standing on ice so crystal thin, it is like touching the wet of an eyeball, and beyond it is yourself, alive and clawing into contact. You tell all this to the next white woman sitting across from you in a fold-up chair—your mother's immigration, your brother's explosive and wasted life, your father's quiet devotion to the dream of you, your resilient love for ballsack and white cock. She touches her wrist: *It seems... you have a lot of problems....* adjusting her watch: *to think about... See you next Monday?* Her thumb pressed on the glass face.

X

All your potatoes on the ground—you were never meant for this. The camerawoman tiptoes around spilled tubers as she zooms in on your front teeth, tearing open a parcel of dried shrimp. Grainlike, pink nymphs packed tight with twenty hundred eyes staring out, punctuating the space between your hands. So assaulted by nostalgia, so aroused by the filth and seafood blast of umami, you can't stop looking at Ted Allen's mouth. It moves. Tell me chef, is there anyone special you're competing for today? This is the moment, your fingers gripped around the handle of your cleaver: "I'm competing today to honor my mother, who taught me everything about sacrifice and generosity through the warmth she carried from the kitchen into her life." At the word "life", you tilt your head up and rock your blade slowly into the heft of a red onion. Then you remember your mother is still alive. A tear slides down your face.

Originally published in *The Margins.*

Wo Chan is a queer Fujianese poet and drag performer. A recipient of fellowships from the Asian American Writers' Workshop, Poets House, Kundiman, and Lambda Literary, Wo's work has been published in *cream city review, Cortland Review, VYM Magazine,* and elsewhere. As a member of Brooklyn-based drag alliance, Switch n' Play, Wo has performed at venues including Brooklyn Pride, The Trevor Project, and the Architectural Digest Expo.

Elegy with Apples, Pomegranates, Bees, Butterflies, Thorn Bushes, Oak, Pine, Warblers, Crows, Ants, and Worms

The trees alongside the fence
bear fruit, the limbs and leaves speeches
to you and me. They promise to give the world
back to itself. The apple apologizes
for those whose hearts bear too much zest
for heaven, the pomegranate
for the change that did not come
soon enough. Every seed is a heart, every heart
a minefield, and the bees and butterflies
swarm the flowers on its grave.
The thorn bushes instruct us
to tell our sons and daughters
who carry sticks and stones
to mend their ways.
The oak tree says to eat
only fruits and vegetables;
the pine says to eat all the stirring things.
My neighbor left long ago and did not hear
any of this. In a big country
the leader warns the leader of a small country
there must be change or else.
Birds are the same way, coming and going,
wobbling thin branches.
The warblers express pain, the crows regret,
or is it the other way around?
The mantra today is the same as yesterday.
We must become different.
The plants must, the animals,
and the ants and worms, just like the carmakers,
the soap makers before them,
and the manufacturers of rubber
and the sellers of tea, tobacco, and salt.
Such an ancient habit, making ourselves new.
My neighbor looks like my mother

who left a long time ago
and did not hear any of this.
Just for a minute, give her back to me,
before she died, kneeling
in the dirt under the sun, calling me darling
in Arabic, which no one has since.

Originally published in *Poem-A-Day*.

Hayan Charara is a poet, children's book author, essayist, and editor. His poetry books are *Something Sinister* (2016), *The Sadness of Others* (2006), and *The Alchemist's Diary* (2001). His children's book, *The Three Lucys* (2016), received the New Voices Award Honor, and he edited *Inclined to Speak* (2008), an anthology of contemporary Arab American poetry. With Fady Joudah, he is also a series editor of the Etel Adnan Poetry Prize. Born in Detroit in 1972 to Arab immigrants, he spent a decade in New York City and in 2004 moved to Texas, where he now lives.

SEAGULL, TINY

The   villagers   are
watchful

in   their   booths   at
boston market

The   boys   living   on
sulfur

and   talking   about
feelings

and   memory   The
united states

is   the   collective
process of

demanding   feelings
and a certain

memory   I would live
on synthetics

but   i   hate   fragility
Lonely and afraid,

my women sing, *there*
is no father

in me   They talk
about anything

a limit allows   There
is hope

of forgiveness, but my
american

corpse has been such
a disappointment

I would live on feeling
safe

and   spilling   secrets
It is confusing

the   plain   people
passing

like potato blossoms
When i first

met a trans person at
age 7

she served us mashed
potatoes

at   boston   market
Mother winced

and   statistically   it's
unlikely she

kept the job. *I am*
worthy

of eating food i tell
myself There

is   some   hope   of
forgiveness

for boys I would live
on their plastic

It is confusing that
words trick us

Originally published in *Feminist Wire* and *Safe Space* (Ahsahta Press, 2016).

Jos Charles is a trans poet and author of *Safe Space* (Ahsahta Press, 2016). They are founding-editor of *THEM: a trans literary journal*. They have writing published (and/or publications forthcoming) with *Denver Quarterly, Washington Square Review, PEN America, Action Yes, GLAAD, LAMBDA Literary,* and elsewhere. Jos Charles received their MFA from the University of Arizona in Tucson where they currently reside.

Woe Are You?

It was hardly war, the hardliest of wars. Hardly, hardly. It occurred to me that this particular war was hardly war because of kids, more kids, those poor kids. The kids were hungry until we GIs fed them. We dusted them with DDT. Hardly done. Rehabilitation of Korea that is. It needs chemical fertilizer from the States, power to build things like a country. In the end it was the hardliest of wars made up of bubble gum, which GIs had to show those kids how to chew. In no circumstance whatever can man be comfortable without art. They don't want everlasting charity, and we are not giving it to them. We are just lending them a hand until they can stand on their own two feet. A novel idea. This is why it occurred to me that this particular war was hardly war, the hardliest of wars.

My father was hardly himself during the war, then I was born during the era that hardly existed, and, therefore, I hardly existed without DDT. Beauty is pleasure regarded as the quality of a thing. I prefer a paper closet with real paper dresses in it. To be born hardly, hardly after the hardliest of wars is a matter of debate. Still going forward. We are, that is. Napalm again. This is the THE BIG PICTURE. War and its masses. War and its men. War and its machines. Together we form THE BIG PICTURE. From Korea to Germany from Alaska to Puerto Rico. All over the world, the US Army is on the alert to defend our country, you the people against aggression. This is THE BIG PICTURE, an official television report to the nation from the army. This is Korea! Is one thing better than another? These South Koreans are alright. Woe is you, woe is war, hardly war, woe is me, woe are you? My father is still alive and this is how I came to prefer a paper closet with real paper dresses in it.

Well, it's morning in Korea. The most violently mountainous place on Earth. Everyone has been dusted, existence hardly done, whereas beauty has been regarded as the quality of a thing. At Uncle Dann's Huddle doughnuts and coffee are free and in case there are any, for there are many, the unescorted ladies are not permitted. The decision has been made in Tokyo for the hardliest of wars, an old soldier made it. The situation in Korea is so critical that we the Navy must give the 8th Army practical support. Do you remember how you began this day? How did you spend this morning? Woe are you? Well, pine cones fall every day. So why do we fail? Miles and miles of homeless refugees set adrift by the Red Scourge.

Some lines borrowed from The Forgotten War, a documentary made up of army footages and narration; "Is one thing better than another?" from Postcard Object (1988) by Allen Ruppersberg at The Henry Art Gallery in 2010; "Beauty is pleasure regarded as the quality of a thing" is by Santayana and "In no circumstance whatever can man be comfortable without art" is by Ruskin.

I Refuse to Translate

무궁화꽃이피었습니다
무궁화꽃이피었습니다
무궁화꽃이피었습니다
무궁화꽃이피었습니다
무궁화꽃이피었습니다

1 2 3 4 5 = 무
1 2 3 4 5 = 궁
1 2 3 4 5 = 화
1 2 3 4 5 = 수
1 2 3 4 5 = 국

I refuse to translate
I refuse to translate
I refuse to translate
I refuse to translate
I refuse to translate

5=Over

A Little Glossary

미=국 수=국 무=국 화=국 애=국

Beauty=Gook Hydrangea=Gook Radish=Gook Flower=Gook Love=Gook

무궁화=5 petals

(후렴) 무 -- 궁 화

Don Mee Choi is the author of *Hardly War* (Wave Books, 2016), *Petite Manifesto – chapbook (Vagabond, 2014), The Morning News Is Exciting* (Action Books, 2010), and translator of contemporary Korean women poets. She has received a Whiting Writers Award and the 2012 Lucien Stryk Translation Prize.

Choi Jeong Min
for my parents, Choi Inyeong & Nam Songeun

In the first grade, I asked my mother permission
to go by Frances at school. At seven years old,

I already knew the exhaustion of hearing my name
butchered by hammerhead tongues. Already knew

to let my salty gook name drag behind me
in the sand, safely out of sight. In fourth grade

I wanted to be a writer & worried
about how to escape my surname – Choi

is nothing if not Korean, if not garlic breath,
if not seaweed & sesame & food stamps

during the lean years – could I go by F.J.C.? Could I be
paper thin & raceless? Dust jacket & coffee stain,

boneless rumor smoldering behind the curtain
& speaking through an ink-stained puppet?

My father ran through all his possible rechristenings –
Ian, Issac, Ivan – & we laughed at each one,

knowing his accent would always give him away.
You can hear the pride in my mother's voice

when she answers the phone *this is Grace.* & it is
some kind of strange grace she's spun herself,

some lightning made of chainmail. Grace is not
her pseudonym, though everyone in my family is a poet.

These are the shields for the names we speak in the dark
to remember our darkness. Savage death rites

we still practice in the new world. Myths we whisper

to each other to keep warm. My Korean name

is the star my mother cooks into the jjigae
to follow home when I am lost, which is always

in this gray country, this violent foster home
whose streets are paved with shame, this factory yard

riddled with bullies ready to steal your skin
& sell it back to your mother for profit,

land where they stuff our throats with soil
& accuse us of gluttony when we learn to swallow.

I confess. I am greedy. I think I deserve to be seen
for what I am: a boundless, burning wick.

A perfect chord. I confess: If someone has looked
at my crooked spine and called it elmwood,

I've accepted. If someone has loved me more
for my gook name, for my saint name,

for my good vocabulary & bad joints,
I've welcomed them into this house.

I've cooked them each a meal with a star singing
at the bottom of the bowl, a secret ingredient

to follow home when we are lost:
sunflower oil, blood sausage, a name

given by a dead grandfather who eventually
forgot everything he'd touched. I promise:

I'll never stop stealing back what's mine.
I promise: I won't forget again.

Originally published in *The Margins.*

Franny Choi is the author of *Floating, Brilliant, Gone* (Write Bloody Publishing, 2014). She has received awards and fellowships from the Poetry Foundation, Kundiman, and the Rhode Island State Council on the Arts. Her work has appeared in *Poetry Magazine, the Poetry Review, Indiana Review, The Journal,* and others. She is an MFA candidate at the University of Michigan, a Project VOICE teaching artist, and a member of the Dark Noise Collective.

Viciousness in Ends

blood and trust   in my mouth
on the ground   sweltering each
swing harder   dizzy still   to protect what?

    inside red and black gloves with quarter-
worn knuckles   part of a man   two fists thick
no way to know the stranger   from my

brother's hand –   the boxing glove   still hot
    past it sticky hand slipping into –
we refused to go   the fear in our throats –

stuck like meat in our teeth   *and it was good*   and it was
    from one another   and sweat genesis and took
uncut grass   we laughed   face down

in the yellow   to press each other's necks   like dull blades
and used our forearms – where he breaks
    we laughed   because we swore   a man is born

into each other's sharp backs   point blank
    we shot the metal bb's   we shot
the metal bb's point blank into each other's

sharp backs   because we swore a man is born
where he breaks   we laughed and used
    our forearms like dull blades   to press each other's

necks face down   in the yellow uncut grass   we laughed
and sweat genesis and took   from one another
and it was good   and it was stuck   like meat

in our teeth the fear   in our throats – we refused
    to go past it sticky hand slipping
into the boxing glove   still hot from my brother's hand –

no way to know the stranger part   of a man two fists thick
        with quarter-worn knuckles   inside red and black
gloves to protect what? each swing harder   dizzy

still   on the ground   sweltering blood   and trust in my mouth

Originally published in *Pinwheel.*

Aaron Coleman is Third Year Fellow in Poetry in Washington University's MFA Program and Public Projects Assistant at Pulitzer Arts Foundation. A Fulbright Scholar from Metro-Detroit, Aaron has lived and worked with youth in locations including Kalamazoo, Chicago, Spain, and South Africa. Winner of the *Tupelo Quarterly* TQ5 Poetry Contest and a semifinalist for the 2015 92Y/Discovery Poetry Contest, his poems have appeared or are forthcoming in *Boston Review, The Greensboro Review, Meridian, Pinwheel, Southern Indiana Review, Tupelo Quarterly,* and elsewhere.

Eduardo C. Corral

Ceremonial

          Delirious,
touch-starved,
        I pinch a mole
              on my skin, pull it
off, like a bead—
        I pinch & pull until
              I am holding
a black rosary. Prayer
        will not cool
              my fever.
Prayer will not
        melt my belly fat,
              will not thin
my thighs.
              A copper-
faced man once
        called me beautiful.
              Stupid,
stupid man.
        I am obese. I am
              worthless.
I can still feel
        his thumb—
              warm,
burled—moving
        in my mouth.
              His thumbnail
a flake
              of sugar
he would not
        allow me to swallow.
              Desperate
for the sting of snow
        on my skin,
              rosary
tight in my fist,

I walk into
        a closet, crawl
into a wedding dress.
        Oh Lord,
here I am.

Originally published in *Poem-A-Day*.

Eduardo C. Corral is the author of *Slow Lightning* (Yale University Press, 2012), which was chosen by Carl Phillips as the 2011 winner of the Yale Series of Younger Poets. He is the recipient of a "Discovery"/The Nation Award, the J. Howard and Barbara M. J. Wood Prize from *Poetry*, a National Endowment for the Arts Fellowship, and a Whiting Award. He lives in New York.

North Node

According to her, I appeared to my mother in an in-utero vision and told her my name. Before I chose my mother, all day long I ran my fingertips along the slick backs of cutthroat trout and gathered water from Mill Creek into a sapphire pale, I waited for her. In the distance there was a blue bull surrounded by lilies.

She loves me so she bore me underwater. I'm here to learn a lesson. I spent my other lives in the Nevada desert, where I only did what felt good. *What could that mean?* I reconcile the pleasure in lying naked on the hot sand of the Mojave, watching the braided muscles in a horse's hind legs, with the ocean nowhere, a frying chest slammed to the hood of an idle car. I'm here to cut the scorpion from my throat. Even though it has dragged me through sweet darkness and time. Even now, in the stillness of home, in love and full of wine, it wraps its eight legs around me. Even through the lilies, it sets its many eyes on me and then longing

Originally published in *The Cortland Review.*

Rio Cortez is a graduate of Sarah Lawrence College and the MFA program at NYU. Her manuscript, *I Have Learned to Define a Field as a Space Between Mountains*, was selected by Ross Gay as the winner of the 2016 inaugural Toi Derricotte & Cornelius Eady Chapbook Prize, and is available from Jai-Lai Books.

Cynthia Cruz

Midnight Office

The child is not dead.
She is sleeping.

Gone from this world
Which is broken.

The angel of Michael
Outside the garden
His circle of fire
Maddening around the tree.

He put the word
Back into her:
A heavy kind of music.

Then she was free.
As we all are.

All night I stood in the icy wind,
Praying for the storm to destroy me.

But the wind blew through me
Like I was a hologram.

If you say I am a mystic,
Then fine: I'm a mystic.

The trees are not trees, anyway.

Originally published in *Poetry*.

Cynthia Cruz is the author of
*Wunderkammer, The
Glimmering Room, and Ruin.*
She has published poems in
numerous literary journals and
magazines including the *New
Yorker, Kenyon Review,* the
Paris Review, and the *Boston
Review,* and in anthologies
including *Isn't it Romantic: 100
Love Poems by Younger Poets,*
and *The Iowa Anthology of
New American Poetrie*s. She is
the recipient of fellowships
from Yaddo, the MacDowell
Colony, and a Hodder fellowship from Princeton University. Cruz teaches writing at Sarah
Lawrence College. She has published essays, interviews, book and art reviews in the *LA
Review of Books, Hyperallergic, Guernica, The American Poetry Review,* and *The Rumpus.*
She lives in Brooklyn.

Kyle Dargan

"The Erotic is a Measure in Between"
~after Lorde

Your body is not my pommel horse
nor my Olympic pool or diving board.
Your body is not my personal internet
channel nor my timeline,
nor my warm Apollo spotlight.
Your body is not my award
gala. Your body is not my game—
preseason or playoffs.
Your body is not my political party
convention. Your body is not
my frontline or my war's theatre.
Your body is not my time
trial. Your body is not my entrance
exam or naturalization interview.
I am a citizen of this skin—that
alone—and yours is not to be
passed nor won. What is done—
when we let our bodies sharpen
the graphite of each other's bodies
—is not my test, not my solo
show. One day I'll learn. I'll prove
I know how to lay with you without
anticipating the scorecards of your eyes,
how I might merely abide—we two
unseated, equidistant from the wings
in a beating black box, all stage.

Originally published in *Poem-A-Day*.

Kyle Dargan is the author of four collections of poetry, *Honest Engine* (2015), *Logorrhea Dementia* (2010), *Bouquet of Hungers* (2007), and *The Listening* (2003)—all published by the University of Georgia Press. He has received the Cave Canem Poetry Prize, the Hurston/Wright Legacy Award, and his books have been finalists for the Kingsley Tufts Poetry Award and the Eric Hoffer Awards Grand Prize.

The New Grief Work

I have walked in the garden
of her wound—: gazed the black flower

        blooming her animal-
        eye, astonished.

Why not now go toward the things I love?

Like Jacob's angel, I touched the garnet
of her hip,

        and she knew my name,
        and I knew hers—:

it was *Auxocromo*, it was *Cromóforo*,
it was *Eliza*.

When the eyes and lips are brushed with honey
what is seen and said will never be the same,

so why not take the apple
in your mouth—

        on flame, in pieces—straight
        from the knife's sharp edge.

Achilles chased Hektor around the walls
of Ilium three times—: how long must I circle

the high gate
between her hip and knee

        to solve the red-gold geometry
        of her thigh?

Again the gods put their large hands in me,
move me, break my heart

like a clay jug of wine, loosen a beast
from some darklong depth—:

my melancholy is hoofed.
I, the terrible beautiful

Lampon, a shining devour-horse tethered
at the bronze manger of her collarbones.

I do my grief work
with her body—:

labor to make the emerald tigers
in her throat leap,

lead them burning green to drink
from the deep-violet jetting her breast,

give up my sorrows
the way a bull gives it horns—:

wishing there is rest
in the body's softest parts.

We go where there is love,

to the river, on our knees beneath the sweet
water. I pull her under four times,

until we are rivered.
We are rearranged.

I wash the silk and silt of her from my hands—:
Now who I come to, I come clean to,

I come good to.

Originally published in *Poem-a-Day*.

Natalie Diaz was born and raised in the Fort Mojave Indian Village in California. She is Mojave and an enrolled member of the Gila River Indian Tribe. Her first poetry collection, *When My Brother Was an Aztec*, was published by Copper Canyon Press. She is a Lannan Literary Fellow and a Native Arts Council Foundation Artist Fellow. She was awarded a Bread Loaf Fellowship, the Holmes National Poetry Prize, a Hodder Fellowship, a PEN/Civitella Ranieri Foundation Residency, and a US Artists Ford Fellowship. Diaz teaches at Arizona State University and the Institute of American Indian Arts. She is working to revitalize the Mojave language.

Tafisha A. Edwards

The Double Blind

VI.

Gin is the tension of the night. Gin is heavy on our tongues.
Our tongues are heavy on each other and flat and limber
and searching. A hand is sneaking in my blouse,

a hand is sneaking in my blouse and this is not embellishment—
you know the way you sneak, that peculiar weight bearing creep,
the circular route of this verb,

the circular route of this verb, this creeping, this questing, this alarm
bell surge in the cortex corridor, this warning, muted by gin
I relax.

I relax. I do not want to be "that girl." That girl takes it
the wrong way. That girl should just let the hand creep.
This is all right.

Is this all right? The mute gin girl relaxes and breathes and counts
bodies on the 3 a.m. sidewalk. Negative 4. Counts the leaves
on the 3 a.m. tree. 64.

On the 3 a.m. tree. 64. 65. 66. 67. 68. 69. 70. 70. 70. 70.
We are at the hour of recrimination. Only legs and wallets
are open after 10.

Only legs and wallets are open after 10. We are five
hours past respectable. Five hours past reasonable.
We are thirty-five minutes from my house.

Thirty-five minutes from my house. A hand snuck in my blouse
and panties and scalp and a questing, a searching, a "You smell
so fucking good,"

so fucking good, this circular route past consent, this gin
heavy quest, my panic on his breath, this being taken
the wrong way

the wrong way, the wrong hour, wrong night, wrong
dress, wrong choice and a terrible pause—

Count the leaves on the 3 a.m. tree. 70. 69. 68. Thirty-five
minutes past

III.

In 48 population-based surveys from around the world 10 – 69% of women reported being physically assaulted by an intimate male partner at some point.

What is more intimate than a fist?
Than the champagne cork
pop
of cartilage and bone?

More than 50% of rapes/sexual assaults occur within 1 mile of home. 4 out of 10 occur at home

is where the heart is   where the heart   is   where

Every two minutes another American is sexually assaulted:

I.

120.

Lifetime rate of rape/attempted rape for women by race:

- *American Indian & Alaskan Women 34.1 %*
- *Mixed Race Women 24.4%*
- *Black Women 18.8%*
- *White Women 17.7%*
- *All Women 17.6%*
- *Asian Pacific Islander Women 6.8%*

"But that's not even 20%. You have a better chance of being hit

by a car."

II.

"They found her right behind the hospital, I saw
the sirens from my window. They heard
her body in the snow. No head. Naked. I think
the guy had raped her. I think. Why not,
at that point? I wanted to stop the contractions.
I wanted to keep you up in me a little bit
longer. You wanted out! Let's go hurry up!
The nurses couldn't stop crying.
They were crying in the hallways.
A nurse was missing. From the hospital.
I don't know if the body was black.
That nurse was black—"

  Are you serious?

"Yeah, it wasn't safe. But the woman,
they never did find out who. I don't even think
they found her head. Or maybe that was the girl
they found in the river in the spring. Or
that housewife in Ottawa. Or that Mississauga girl.
Young like you. 19. Or that pregnant single
mom. Belly big with the sixth baby when
the boyfriend kill her. Or that other woman.
Her husband beat her in the middle of the day
with a hammer. Airi, I think was her name. Yeah.
That was a bad year for women."

I.

What were you wearing on the night of the attack?

How short was your skirt on the night of the attack?

You have underwear on   on the night of the attack?

How sheer was the garment on the night of the attack?

Can you name your attacker?

Could you spell that?

Were you romantically involved before the night of the attack?

And after?

So, you were romantically involved before the night of the attack.

Would you say he was a good boyfriend?

Can you tell me why your relationship came to an end?

And why did you decide to see him again?

Did you flirt with him on the "night of the attack?"

Did you drink with him on the "night of the attack?"

Were you in a bad mood before "the attack?"

Did you feel any pleasure during "the attack?"

        Are you sure there even was

Originally published in The Offing.

Tafisha A. Edwards can make a great cup of Love Potion #10. She is the author of *THE BLOODLET*, winner of Phantom Books' 2016 Breitling Chapbook Prize. Her work has appeared in *The Offing*, *PHANTOM*, *Gigantic Sequins*, *Bodega Magazine*, *Fjords Review*, *The Little Patuxent Review*, and other print and online publications. She is a graduate of the University of Maryland's Jiminéz-Porter Writers' House, a Cave Canem fellow, and a former educator with the American Poetry Museum. She is the recipient of a Zoland Poetry Fellowship from the Vermont Studio Center and has received scholarships to The Juniper Summer Writing Institute, The Minnesota Northwoods Writers' Conference and other writing workshops and conferences. She is currently writing her first collection of poetry, *Confusing the Wind*.

Before A Future Generation

Of necessity, I have learned to navigate
        the junkyard of my own viscera.

The butcher arranges my bones, desires
        the hairs on a slabbed kneecap.

The body is another kind of evening
        under infrared lights. She segments

my belly: I am so skinny no skin
        can hurt me. I am the impression

of wind through the fur of a maimed gazelle.
        The butcher she tends to my gashes

to make them bloodless, my neck bone a dressage
        she will hold and make proper again.

To be sexless finally, to be meat,
        she places a lemon between my lips,

freshens them into a pucker to kiss
        like the beak of a parrot fish. A man

from the village peers into the shop
        eager to touch me between parchment,

a man who laid me down in faux down
        to deliver me my kingdom of filth

and hunger. My butcher she flattens my belly,
        to be sliced is to be seen importantly,

bright tower in a failed city. She did this sipping
        iced coffee through a straw, a Baltic song

stopped in her head. My thigh's modern coldness
        on the counter. You will come to know this was love.

Originally published in *The Paris American.*

The Limits of What We Can Do

Neutrality is a privilege. The rocks we throw
ourselves onto are a privilege. It is hard to hate
creation on the first day of warmth, but I am vigilant
and a sac still fills up my mother and a sac fills up
my father and a sac deflates my grandmother
and I have no sense of sac. Tory Dent describes
her slow dying as "sham orgasms" and I'm thinking
of expansion, how I read HIV, Mon Amour first in the sun on a day
in May with my beach-body and my coffee to stay.
I know what I'm doing with this poem is a sham
the way I knew I knew my vivacious privilege
was a portrait of a bad institution, capitalism fingered
my throat with its delicious incentives of eat
and I did eat because I had touched love and love knew what to do
with me. I like poetry because there are no miracles in it,
it is like the dream I had about disease nestled marked
curled as a burst blood vessel in the eyeball, that to own
up to the mark was to look up inside your skull for others to see it.
The poem is doomed and swimming in fluid.
In my dream I wrote an article for Slate called "The Limits
of What We Can Do" in the face of annihilation
and it was received well. I wake up nestled marked curled
like clickbait, a deep-sea fishing net. I throw up yarn
and go for a run. A love inside of me is breaking.

Originally published in *The New Yorker.*

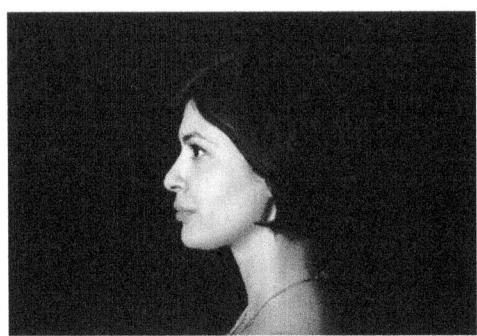

Natalie Eilbert is the author of the debut poetry collection *Swan Feast* (Bloof Books, 2015). She is also the author of two chapbooks, *Conversation with the Stone Wife* (Bloof Books, 2014) and *And I Shall Again Be Virtuous* (Big Lucks Books, 2014). Her work has appeared in or is forthcoming from *The New Yorker, jubilat, Tin House, The Kenyon Review, Sixth Finch,* and elsewhere. She is the founding editor of *The Atlas Review.*

Joshua Jennifer Espinoza

I Dream Of Horses Eating Cops

i dream of horses eating cops
i have so much hope for the future

or no i don't

who knows the sound a head makes when it is asleep
my dad was a demon but so was the white man in uniform
who harassed him for the crime of being brown

there are demons everywhere
dad said
and he was right but not in the way he meant it

the sky over san bernardino was a brilliant blue when the winds kicked in
all the fences and trash cans and smog scattered themselves
and the mountains were on fire every day

i couldn't wait to die or be killed
my woman body trapped in a dream

i couldn't wait to wake up
and ride off into the sunset
but there isn't much that is new anywhere

the same violence swallows itself and produces bodies
and names for bodies

i name my body girl of my dreams
i name my body proximity
i name my body full of hope despite everything
i name my body dead girl who hasn't died yet

i hope i come back as an elephant
i hope we all come back as animals
and eat our fill

i hope everyone gets everything they deserve

Originally published in *Nepantla: A Journal Dedicated to Queer Poets of Color.*

THE MOON IS TRANS

The moon is trans.

From this moment forward, the moon is trans.

You don't get to write about the moon anymore unless you respect that.

You don't get to talk to the moon anymore unless you use her correct pronouns.

You don't get to send men to the moon anymore unless their job is

to bow down before her and apologize for the sins of the earth.

She is waiting for you, pulling at you softly,

telling you to shut the fuck up already please.

Scientists theorize the moon was once a part of the earth

that broke off when another planet struck it.

Eve came from Adam's rib.

Etc.

Do you believe in the power of not listening

to the inside of your own head?

I believe in the power of you not listening

to the inside of your own head.

This is all upside down.

We should be talking about the ways that blood

is similar to the part of outer space between the earth and the moon

but we're busy drawing it instead.

The moon is often described as dead, though she is very much alive.

The moon has not known the feeling of not wanting to be dead

for any extended period of time

in all of her existence, but

she is not delicate and she is not weak.

She is constantly moving away from you the only way she can.

She never turns her face from you because of what you might do.

She will outlive everything you know.

Originally published in *The Feminist Wire.*

Joshua Jennifer Espinoza is a trans woman poet living in California. Her work has been published in *The Offing, The Feminist Wire, Alice Blue,* and elsewhere. Her first book *I'm Alive / It Hurts / I Love It* was released by Boost House in 2014, and her full length collection *There Should Be Flowers* was published in 2016 by Civil Coping Mechanisms.

t'ai freedom ford

this poem is called Beyoncé is a white woman

hot is the new chocolate   chocolate
is the new brown   brown is the new doo-doo
doo-doo is the new shit   shiiiiit is the new
news who knew? know is the new ignorant
ignorant is the old nigger   nigga
is the new black   black is the new orange
orange you glad your black ass ain't in jail?
jail is the new plantation   plantation
is the old blues   blue is the new ivy
league   Blue Ivy is the new envy Be
yonce is the new body new baby
mama the new feminist airbrushed white
white is the new blood blue blood old blood beige
beige is the new rage the new whiteblack blood

Originally published in *Eleven Eleven: A Journal of Literature & Art.*

i know you are but what am i?
for Raven Symone

not African American either
except when being American gets
mistaken for black   for unpredictable
for gun   in the foreground   forced to the ground
for being brown   for Brown versus Board of Ed
for bullets to the forehead—for us   by us
O beautiful for spacious skies for amber
waves of grain O beautiful for faceless
cries for amber graves of pain   for African
blood that remains despite your American
claims for citizenshit—forbidden love hidden
for master get his whip or his dick   forced
fucks foreshadow foreplay   for jungle fever
forever remember: twas them Africans made you
formidable   unfuckwitable   lest you forget

Originally published in *Eleven Eleven: A Journal of Literature & Art*.

t'ai freedom ford is a New York City high school English teacher and Cave Canem Fellow. Her first poetry collection, *how to get over* is forthcoming from *Red Hen Press* in Spring 2017. t'ai lives and loves in Brooklyn, but hangs out digitally at shesaidword.com.

Sarah Gambito

I Am Not from the Philippines

A white guy liked me and it was like
a lake might bend in half.

I wanted to go to The Olive Garden.
I said Yes with my eyes like platelets.

When God was Filipino,
he put a pig and fire together and called it porkissimo.

I grabbed a Filipino girl's hand and she said are you a lesbian.
I faked it to myself. I faked it to them all.

All the nurses ever, ever in the world
are Filipino.

Like a push in the gut, I rush past the hovels of hospital rooms.
The great digital of machines and humans simmering at work.

The pork chop of the leg poking from the blanket.
There will always be sick people. You'll always have a job.

Nurses with their white soft shoes. Their cuneiform writing.
The change purses of nurses diveting around.

My aunts, mothers, uncles, cousins whiplashing into nurses.

Originally published in *Harvard Review Online*.

Sarah Gambito is the author of the poetry collections *Delivered* (Persea Books) and *Matadora* (Alice James Books). Her poems have appeared or are forthcoming in *The Iowa Review, Colorado Review, Denver Quarterly, The New Republic,* and other journals. She is Associate Professor of English / Director of Creative Writing at Fordham University and cofounder of Kundiman, a non-profit organization serving Asian American writers.

And Be

seek and be otherwise occupied, too busy for both devil and god, on and onward. no time to turn back, behind, where only salt and cinders remain as steam, gas, oil, gears, pistons pound in electric horizons, neon stars spelling out omens in the shadow of giants dead on the strip, the main drag where myths are made, live and forgotten to all but the shamans, bards, and oldest of old folk who knew firsthand how little glory there were in those gold and silver days.

spend and share alike. too generous to hate. too generous to envy. too this to be that. too to to be.

all the one way streets towards some to – some at. no other way streets. two ways where this binary is not that binary but however white one grey is some second chance is given to black.

this was proud of that restless forgetfulness as eternity tried to grasp an understanding of 'wait.'

pain and feelings otherwise occupied. too consumed for sin or enlightenment. in and inward. novelty of the past found again in the shortage of youth.

Originally published in *The Brooklyn Rail.*

Kenyatta JP Garcia is the author of several books including: *This Sentimental Education, ROBOT,* and *Playing Dead.* They were raised in Brooklyn, NY before moving to Albany, NY where they received a degree in linguistics. In addition, Garcia spent a dozen years as a cook and currently spends their nights being paid to put boxes on shelves while using the daylight hours to write poetry and humor, read lots of comic books and edit *Horse Less Review.*

Catalog of Unabashed Gratitude

Friends, will you bear with me today,
for I have awakened
from a dream in which a robin
made with its shabby wings a kind of veil
behind which it shimmied and stomped something from the south
of Spain, its breast a'flare,
looking me dead in the eye
from the branch that grew into my window,
coochie-cooing my chin,
the bird shuffling its little talons left, then right,
while the leaves bristled
against the plaster wall, two of them drifting
onto my blanket while the bird
opened and closed its wings like a matador
giving up on murder,
jutting its beak, turning a circle,
and flashing, again,
the ruddy bombast of its breast
by which I knew upon waking
it was telling me
in no uncertain terms
to bellow forth the tubas and sousaphones,
the whole rusty brass band of gratitude
not quite dormant in my belly —
it said so in a human voice,
"Bellow forth" —
and who among us could ignore such odd
and precise counsel?

Hear ye! hear ye! I am here
to holler that I have hauled tons — by which I don't mean lots,
I mean *tons* — of cowshit
and stood ankle deep in swales of maggots
swirling the spent beer grains
the brewery man was good enough to dump off
holding his nose, for they smell very bad,
though make the compost writhe giddy and lick its lips,
twirling dung with my pitchfork
again and again

with hundreds and hundreds of other people,
we dreamt an orchard this way,
furrowing our brows,
and hauling our wheelbarrows,
and sweating through our shirts,
and two years later there was a party
at which trees were sunk into the well-fed earth,
one of which, a liberty apple, after being watered in
was tamped by a baby barefoot
with a bow hanging in her hair
biting her lip in her joyous work
and friends this is the realest place I know,
you could ride your bike there
or roller skate or catch the bus
there is a fence and a gate twisted by hand,
there is a fig tree taller than you in Indiana,
it will make you gasp.
It might make you want to stay alive even, thank you;

and thank you
for not taking my pal when the engine
of his mind dragged him
to swig fistfulls of Xanax and a bottle or two of booze,
and thank you for taking my father
a few years after his own father went down thank you
mercy, mercy, thank you
for not smoking meth with your mother
oh thank you thank you
for leaving and for coming back,
and thank you for what inside my friends'
love bursts like a throng of roadside goldenrod
gleaming into the world,
likely hauling a shovel with her
like one named Aralee ought,
with hands big as a horse's,
and who, like one named Aralee ought,
will laugh time to time til the juice
runs from her nose; oh
thank you
for the way a small thing's wail makes
the milk or what once was milk
in us gather into horses
huckle-buckling across a field;

and thank you, friends, when last spring
the hyacinth bells rang

and the crocuses flaunted
their upturned skirts, and a quiet roved
the beehive which when I entered
were snugged two or three dead
fist-sized clutches of bees between the frames,
almost clinging to one another,
this one's tiny head pushed
into another's tiny wing,
one's forelegs resting on another's face,
the translucent paper of their wings fluttering
beneath my breath and when
a few dropped to the frames beneath:
honey; and after falling down to cry,
everything's glacial shine.

And thank *you*, too. And thanks
for the corduroy couch I have put you on.
Put your feet up. Here's a light blanket,
a pillow, dear one,
for I can feel this is going to be long.
I can't stop
my gratitude, which includes, dear reader,
you, for staying here with me,
for moving your lips just so as I speak.
Here is a cup of tea. I have spooned honey into it.

And thank you the tiny bee's shadow
perusing these words as I write them.
And the way my love talks quietly
when in the hive,
so quietly, in fact, you cannot hear her
but only notice barely her lips moving
in conversation. Thank you what does not scare her
in me, but makes her reach my way. Thank you the love
she is which hurts sometimes. And the time
she misremembered elephants
in one of my poems which, oh, here
they come, garlanded with morning glory and wisteria
blooms, trombones all the way down to the river.
Thank you the quiet
in which the river bends around the elephant's
solemn trunk, polishing stones, floating
on its gentle back
the flock of geese flying overhead.

And to the quick and gentle flocking

of men to the old lady falling down
on the corner of Fairmount and 18th, holding patiently
with the softest parts of their hands
her cane and purple hat,
gathering for her the contents of her purse
and touching her shoulder and elbow;
thank you the cockeyed court
on which in a half-court 3 v 3 we oldheads
made of some runny-nosed kids
a shambles, and the 61-year-old
after flipping a reverse lay-up off a back door cut
from my no-look pass to seal the game
ripped off his shirt and threw punches at the gods
and hollered at the kids to admire the pacemaker's scar
grinning across his chest; thank you
the glad accordion's wheeze
in the chest; thank you the bagpipes.

Thank you to the woman barefoot in a gaudy dress
for stopping her car in the middle of the road
and the tractor trailer behind her, and the van behind it,
whisking a turtle off the road.
Thank you god of gaudy.
Thank you paisley panties.
Thank you the organ up my dress.
Thank you the sheer dress you wore kneeling in my dream
at the creek's edge and the light
swimming through it. The koi kissing
halos into the glassy air.
The room in my mind with the blinds drawn
where we nearly injure each other
crawling into the shawl of the other's body.
Thank you say it plain:
fuck each other dumb.

And you, again, you, for the true kindness
it has been for you to remain awake
with me like this, nodding time to time
and making that noise which I take to mean
yes, or, *I understand*, or, *please go on
but not too long*, or, *why are you spitting
so much*, or, *easy Tiger
hands to yourself.* I am excitable.
I am sorry. I am grateful.
I just want us to be friends now, forever.
Take this bowl of blackberries from the garden.

The sun has made them warm.
I picked them just for you. I promise
I will try to stay on my side of the couch.

And thank you the baggie of dreadlocks I found in a drawer
while washing and folding the clothes of our murdered friend;
the photo in which his arm slung
around the sign to "the trail of silences"; thank you
the way before he died he held
his hands open to us; for coming back
in a waft of incense or in the shape of a boy
in another city looking
from between his mother's legs,
or disappearing into the stacks after brushing by;
for moseying back in dreams where,
seeing us lost and scared
he put his hand on our shoulders
and pointed us to the temple across town;

and thank you to the man all night long
hosing a mist on his early-bloomed
peach tree so that the hard frost
not waste the crop, the ice
in his beard and the ghosts
lifting from him when the warming sun
told him *sleep now*; thank you
the ancestor who loved you
before she knew you
by smuggling seeds into her braid for the long
journey, who loved you
before he knew you by putting
a walnut tree in the ground, who loved you
before she knew you by not slaughtering
the land; thank you
who did not bulldoze the ancient grove
of dates and olives,
who sailed his keys into the ocean
and walked softly home; who did not fire, who did not
plunge the head into the toilet, who said *stop*,
don't do that; who lifted some broken
someone up; who volunteered
the way a plant birthed of the reseeding plant
is called a *volunteer*, like the plum tree
that marched beside the raised bed
in my garden, like the arugula that marched
itself between the blueberries,

84

nary a bayonette, nary an army, nary a nation,
which usage of the word volunteer
familiar to gardeners the wide world
made my pal shout "Oh!" and dance
and plunge his knuckles
into the lush soil before gobbling two strawberries
and digging a song from his guitar
made of wood from a tree someone planted, thank you;

thank you zinnia, and gooseberry, rudbeckia
and pawpaw, Ashmead's kernel, cockscomb
and scarlet runner, feverfew and lemonbalm;
thank you knitbone and sweetgrass and sunchoke
and false indigo whose petals stammered apart
by bumblebees good lord please give me a minute;
and moonglow and catkin and crookneck
and painted tongue and seedpod and johnny jump-up;
thank you what in us rackets glad
what gladrackets us;

and thank you, too, this knuckleheaded heart, this pelican heart,
this gap-toothed heart flinging open its gaudy maw
to the sky, oh clumsy, oh bumblefucked,
oh giddy, oh dumbstruck,
oh rickshaw, oh goat twisting
its head at me from my peach tree's highest branch,
balanced impossibly gobbling the last fruit,
its tongue working like an engine,
a lone sweet drop tumbling by some miracle
into my mouth like the smell of someone I've loved;
heart like an elephant screaming
at the bones of its dead;
heart like the lady on the bus
dressed head to toe in gold, the sun
shivering her shiny boots, singing
Erykah Badu to herself
leaning her head against the window;

and thank you the way my father one time came back in a dream
by plucking the two cables beneath my chin
like a bass fiddle's strings
and played me until I woke singing,
no kidding, singing, smiling,
thank you, thank you,
stumbling into the garden where
the Juneberry's flowers had burst open

like the bells of French horns, the lily
my mother and I planted oozed into the air,
the bazillion ants labored in their earthen workshops
below, the collard greens waved in the wind
like the sails of ships, and the wasps
swam in the mint bloom's viscous swill;

and you, again you, for hanging tight, dear friend.
I know I can be long winded sometimes.
I want so badly to rub the sponge of gratitude
over every last thing, including you, which, yes, awkward,
the suds in your ear and armpit, the little sparkling gems
slipping into your eye. Soon it will be over,

which is precisely what the child in my dream said,
holding my hand, pointing at the roiling sea and the sky
hurtling our way like so many buffalo,
who said *it's much worse than we think,
and sooner,* to whom I said
no duh child in my dreams, what do you think
this singing and shuddering is,
what this screaming and reaching and dancing
and crying is, other than loving
what every second goes away?
Goodbye, I mean to say.
And thank you. Every day.

Ross Gay is the author of *Against Which* (CavanKerry, 2006), *Bringing the Shovel Down* (University of Pittsburgh, 2011), and *Catalog of Unabashed Gratitude* (University of Pittsburgh, 2015). He's also the co-author, with Aimee Nezhukumatathil, of *Pyrite and Lace: Letters from Two Gardens* (Organic Weapon Arts, 2014). He is one of the editors of the online sports magazine, *Some Call It Ballin'*, and he's doing some other really fun stuff. He teaches at Indiana University in Bloomington.

Good Death

Of words placed in their best black clothes. Of that darkness full.
Of the laugh, forged of dust that spilled its gold light into her tomb.
Of the wreath carved upon her copper vault.
Of the ivory city – bones like trumpets – blowing you away from us in song.
Of the city again where you will be welcomed by doves & vultures.
Of the road between the dates, a short slash. An usher in a gold hat.
Of the pronunciation of sorrow always – for me now – in summer.
Of the snake who suffered the story of knowledge.
Of the afterlife & its downpour of ordinary rites.
Of rites I enact in my broken thoughts.
Of my fever waving its anguish until the match goes out in disbelief.
Of the nine stars in Charleston bleeding
        mercy beneath the roof of God.
Of God, God, & God.
Of the peace & suffering my people have been promised.
Of the clean, white clothes I gave the undertaker.
                Here are the stockings, I said, not knowing
whether they would match her skin.
Of the poems I've been trying to write. Die, I say.
        Go elsewhere for songs.
Of the food & the appetite.
Of my father's shoulders in a black suit.
Of downpour again.
Of the animals who charge me with horns
        when I offer my pentameter of ribs.
Of her visitations.
Of the hot comb I cradled on my knees in the bathroom.
Of the brutal gospel of hair, untouched toothbrush, clothes
        in closets with sale tags.
Of dreams where my teeth scatter like maple leaves.
Of what I will never remember.
Of the rain that makes my howls float like empty bottles of glass.
Of the dreams where my white clothes grow flames.
Of what I will remember remembering.
Of the neon-colored nail polish on her hand
        I held at her deathbed.
Of what I hated to ask the night & gods.
Of the knees that remember the orange mud before the grass grew back.
Of you, Reader, looking at my face here & reading me

because we all want to know how to bear it.
Of the strange, caring question their voices poured like grace
        over my side where I was trying to leave. Get out of skin.
Of it being over, again & again.
Of it beginning. They ask me was it a good death, was it
        a good death, was there peace for all of us. Why
        should I want peace instead of my mother?
Of the mothers who have always known while holding children
        in their wombs – why wasn't I told?
Now I walk into the sea with my jewel of anguish & shake those human flowers
        from my new, bald skull.

Originally published in *American Poetry Review*.

Rachel Eliza Griffiths is a poet and visual artist. Her fourth collection, *Lighting the Shadow*, was published by Four Way Books in 2015. Griffiths teaches creative writing at the Institute of American Indian Studies and Sarah Lawrence College. She lives in Brooklyn, New York.

Shapewear

A body is matter to be molded
By use of whale bone and lace or
By taking a body for long walks

There are ways to file one down
To make a body a better shape
Not this boring shrub fruit

Try an hourglass if you want to
Remind a man of his mortality

Best to become a clock
The sands of time will get up inside you
Each time you are picked up and turned over

You will always be itching
Never mind the home remedies
Some men like to have a project
To hammer away at

Did you know some women are shaped like bananas
I have never seen one myself
In the wild

Only as Figure 3. in a state-approved textbook
Because they teach this stuff in health class
To lead girls into their own dysmorphia

You are what you eat
So from now on I am surviving on spunk
I want to possess whatever allows you to be bold
Without getting called feisty

My gut reaction when I am in the world
Is to apologize whether or not I am sorry

No one's ever said sorry to me
For making my eyelashes stick together
With their egg on my face

I am doll eyes I need a doll waist
I make a lovely figure with what I've been given
When I encase my body in exoskeleton

This is how I want
To be looked at but not seen

Who decides what the body absorbs
Versus what it reflects

And how are our bodies not
The most boring thing about us
By now

I would starve mine to transcend
Or shuffle off
If I knew you wouldn't find it cute

I would stand naked at the altar
In the name of the Patriarchy
In the name of its Sons
In the name of the Spirit of Capitalism

When can we retire the syllogism
Time is money is the root of evil
We all know that women are the root

And the dirt and the stem and the bulb

We are ripe swelling fruits
Carrying the seeds
Of our mutually assured destruction

The ways in which we fuck each other up
Let me count them
They are endless fluffy sheep
Bedding me for beauty rest

Originally published in *H_NGM_N*.

Sarah Jean Grimm is a publicist at Penguin Random House and co-founder of the online poetry quarterly, *Powder Keg Magazine*. Her work has appeared in the *Atlas Review, Cosmonauts Avenue, Jellyfish Magazine, Lifted Brown, Sixth Finch*, and elsewhere.

B.B.P. Hosmillo

Born with a War Heart Called "Nostalgia"

A couple of years later I lifted the black sea to my face only to smell your reflection,
　　　　　　it's more like an experience than an image, it's how I moved
my chemical bones to the incensed slow fire that gives birth to fossils
　　　　　　without sex. Here, time watches how everybody has lost everything.
No men hiding in the pouches of the earth. No jungle where blankets of fallen leaves
　　unfold in the name of love that is sometimes, intriguingly, a synonym of country.
Here, the question of all who left that stayed: *what must I do to a reflection*
　　　　whose house I certainly cannot enter but one that is mine?
My idea is not to say it's a reflection. My idea is not to say anything. My idea is not
　of yours, which means in front me is a door, something like abortion blood,
　　　　something to whom I am unfamiliar.

You once said the civilized world comprehends life as dungeon of secrets.
That's why I pass by every house as if I'm not naked, I pretend I'm keeping myself
　　only to myself.　That when someone I don't see follows me is when I'm alive.
Staircases don't always mean *a philanthropist with a box of solution waiting for you*
　　　　　　but that something else is down there or up there.
It seems I have a choice: basement or rooftop, underground or ceiling, to drown or
　　　　　　to tell the torturer where you're hiding.
I've been in all this. I'm a witness, and have I told you that I tried many times
　to forget? It's like reading a book on terror
　　　　and of course I saw your name written in quotation, italicized, in bold and
someone with a gun imported from America asked me *who is your lover?* and I said
　　　　　　let me read this again to be sure.

Originally published in *Cha: An Asian Literary Journal.*

B.B.P. Hosmillo is a queer poet of color. He is the author of two forthcoming books, *The Essential Ruin* and *Breed Me: a Sentence without a Subject*; the latter due in late 2016 by AJAR Press with Vietnamese translation by Hanoi-based poets Nhã Thuyên and Kaitlin Rees. His writing has appeared in *Borderlands: Texas Poetry Review, The Margins, Kritika Kultura, Alice Blue,* and *Subprimal Poetry Art,* among others. He received scholarships and research fellowships from the Japan Foundation, Asia Research Institute at the National University of Singapore, and the Republic of Indonesia. He is guest poetry editor at *Cha: An Asian Literary Journal,* an English publication based in Hong Kong.

Brenda Iijima

Earth what to do with us use

Earth what to do with us use
patrol living sanctuary the campus of resistance
cops are employed by the state to serve some us that can't be
seen the us of houses of epistemological space intrinsic political organization
camped out by the domestic policy
crying into the glass
while discussing this project of the world
they think like money
and use us finality
degrade the mission
this fucking matters
as does here-ness over and again
here carnage + primal scene
how disaster melds with body ecology
forms of rebellion the body takes
cops don't sense the dialogue
locked into cue from deep state mandate
our state of mind—psychotopological
each cop an accessory of violent intention
colonizing with automatic weapons
suction assimilationist white holes
making here incapable of love, hope
and transformational resistance

sprawling carceral state
body is a social apparatus
lockdown inside and out
trapped in digital proliferation
and heavy weaponry
we ate what was thrown away

Originally published in *Colorado Review.*

Brenda Iijima is the author, most recently, of *Untimely Death is Driven Out Beyond the Horizon* (1913 Press, 2015) and *Early Linoleum* (Counterpath Press, 2015). She runs Portable Press @ Yo-Yo Labs and lives in Brooklyn, NY.

MUTATIONS AND DELETIONS (3): For Ban

To make: "…a turn to what Ernst Bloch would call the not-yet-conscious or the-not-yet-here." – **José Esteban Muñoz**, *Living the Wrong Life Otherwise* (Social Text: January 13th, 2013.)

Because I wrote Ban on my blog like a finger. And because, at the last possible moment, I pressed click.

Deletion 1:

It's not that I didn't write a novel; it's that I did not publish it. At the last moment, I deleted it.

Am I exaggerating? Perhaps I am under-exaggerating.

I wake up in Delhi, for example, focusing upon the freshly dyed black wool hanging from a line in the garden and dripping, observed through the netting of the door.

The door. The net. The grid.

The garden with its triptych of fuchsia, green, and black.

Complicated zig-zag stems.

Mutation 1:

It is my fifth or sixth morning in Delhi, and for some reason, I have put off visiting the site where "Nirbhaya" – The Fearless One – or: "Damini" – Lightning – died. Partly it is that I am staying with my aunt and uncle in Vasunt Kunj. "Why do you want to go there? This is dirty stuff," says my uncle in Punjabi, showing me an uplifting clip from The Ellen Show on his mobile phone.

There's a complexity to how the morning will go. First we fetch the milk. Then boil it. Then it's too hot. Or perhaps we are drinking tea. Or perhaps it is night. And the night-blooming jasmine is in bloom. Yet, at the end of my first week, I hire a taxi and go to the part [split] in the road where the Mahipalpur Flyover splits to become, also, a service road running alongside, through the market toward the garden center or "nursery." When I arrive, a bright orange light flares then suppresses, or so it seems: itself. A low, toxic-smelling fog has turned everything white. The taxi driver is nervous. I stand for a few minutes outside Hotel 37, nervous, re-thinking my outfit – a scarlet and gold silk kurta with ski pants – trying to breathe. A crowd of men gathers, curious, neutral at this stage, though by the time I pour the red powder on the ground – the site, that is, of some of the most extreme, abandoned gender violence even this country has seen in a long time – the men begin to stir, irritated. They are not smiling. The doorman comes down from the step of the hotel and stands next to me, indicating the notebook tucked beneath my arm: "Madam? Are you doing a survey?"

It is a regular spiral-bound notebook, wide ruled. 70 pages.

Was it this doorman, I think, who brought the white sheet from the hotel and threw it over the denuded [dismembered] body of Jyoti Singh Pandey and her partner, who lay, also, flailing, there, on the dirt where I now am, for forty minutes, before any one of these people – bystanders – called the police? In the death sentence judgment, this sheet is ripped in half. Who did that? Did they use their teeth? Before it was thrown over. The two: forms.

The taxi driver is anxious, the doorman is anxious. Nothing can happen here today, I realize, and also: nothing is here. I had imagined flowers and graffiti, as per the memorials at the Munirka Bus Stand, where Pandey boarded the bus – where – she was [would be]: decimated. But there's nothing here, at the place where she was thrown from the bus, and the men who have gathered to watch – men loosened from the nearby *paan* stand – are chewing something. Two of them are biting off chunks of sugarcane, a typical snack. As I walk back to the taxi, something hits the back of my head, and then something else – my leg.

Chewed up, sucked dry sugarcane. Aimed. The thing I ate as a child on the long: sojourns. In 1970s and 1980s Punjab.

It's not this visit but a subsequent one – in which I reach down and get [retrieve] some of the asphalt chunks, street dirt, fold it in a piece of paper and put it in my bag. Many months later, in Montana, at a conference on race and creative writing, I will eat it. I will eat a chunk of the floor of the world. An ancient practice from my home culture that I feel safe enough to share with the other brown and black people of the conference, though – at another conference, in Los Angeles – I stall and recede from – a depiction.

Of what it could be.

To eat the floor.

And thus to break it down. To be processed: by my own filters or organ meats. Are they fins? Are they screens?

Then discharged. A form, you could say, of assimilation. Oh shut up. Oh go back to England.

Originally published in *documenta 14*.

Bhanu Kapil has written through the cyborg, the monster, the humanimal – and other forms. Her most recent works comprise a diptych: *Schizophrene* and *Ban en Banlieue*, both from Nightboat Books.

NG: Grunt Grammaticality

Please play Branford Marsalis's recording "Berta, Berta" off *I Heard You Twice the First Time*—attend closely the 1:40 mark.

Consider, next, "NG." But more "NG" later.

Here's a memory: poet and critic Duriel Estelle Harris at the Association of Writers and Writing Programs Conference in Boston (2013). On the panel, "Embracing the Verb of It: Black Poets Innovating," I recall Harris hucking a ruck of sound down the chuck well of her gullet—wet sound, flesh sound of hawked spit backed-up, the gag switch booting it back down against her breath.

Again, song: The JB's "The Grunt," which squalls out, hauls off on your ear, from scream, to complaint, into *this riff, this riff.*

A riff I first heard here: Public Enemy's "Night of the Living Baseheads" (from *It Takes a Nation of Millions to Hold Us Back*)—a song that begins with an indictment of a historic trauma that's still here, still now. The riff of the Grunt rendered an alarm by The Bomb Squad.

The Grunt isn't talk. Perhaps it's the utter
utterance, ancestor of mutter, mother tongue of sensation. Uncouth. Fuck sound, the Grunt, mouth stuffed with chewed food sound, shitting sound. A sound of struggle to take in and/or get out, dumb sound. The tongue that grunts is a slug of meat, not the agile quill of "the articulate."

In this, the Grunt—a dineffable techne—resists writing, shows up outlantish on a white sheet of paper, look at it, just look at it. It appears cut out itself into a stage direction—*she* [grunts]—or as a typo, *mm-MM, hhhuh, NG!* All that language and then that Grunt—a gesture toward a signification of authenticity—a brass tacks tactic that says listen to it, just listen to it.

But that's not why I'm interested in the Grunt.
Authentic compared to what? Outlantish to where? No, I stay studying the Grunt for its capacity as a marker of resistance, because of its dintelligibility—or legibility as noise among noises and thus, its signal. I'm studying it and making studies of it, via questions of typography and performance, to locate it ultimately in a syntax.

The Grunt marks resistance—it is the prefix that means "too" and "two": it's too good; it's too hard; it's too much. And the two of the two, are the "it" and the "I." *It's* too much for *me. It's* too hard for *me. It's* too good for *me.* To take in, to take on, to accept, to say no, to consider and, as such, too hard, too good, too much to let out. The Grunt a noisy signal of extremis.

But dintelligibility is, to some, ambiguous, as can be the Grunt—that "too" might be vernacular, running a not-bad-meaning-bad-but-bad-meaning-good thus a carnival somersault—

but one that mis-lands. For the affirmative Grunt is a monomorphemic "in spite of." The affirmative Grunt says: "It's too much for me *but* I'll go on." The affirmative Grunt's ambiguity: whom of the two does "in spite of" serve?

And extremis in service of another is complicated. Heroic? Cowardly? Messianic? Servile? Massachistic? NG. The affirmative Grunt signifies resistance and flexibility. It stretches to accommodate.

But to accommodate what? A dominance? Perhaps systemic, perhaps temporary, perhaps permitted? Yet, I'd speak here briefly about Speech as an assertion of dominance in the face of a grunt that may not be affirmative:

Don't you grunt at me! Use your words.
Don't talk with your mouth full.
Say my name! Say my name!
What the hell did you just say?

These commands rebuke grunts that resist an articulation. Yet such grunts articulate—a double-jointed finger bends "wrong" but it bends. This is the Grunt that appears well-nigh zanily in the text. "Speak!" we read at it. In the sudden resolution of writing to a type-set sequence of letters, the Grunt on the page becomes typography. We see it. We sound it out. We become aware we are reading. The Grunt shunts us out the text—imagining ourselves suddenly having a stereophonic experience, different somehow, than the lubricated silence of reading. A performance, thus a body, and bodies eat, fuck, shit—it's too much.

I am interested in dintelligibility and a syntax of Grunt. I think of grunt-on-grunt—a site in which resistance is interrogated. A police officer beats someone with a baton. The effort is strenuous. The batonier grunts with it, abandoning words like "stop" or "no" or "please." The batoned, also making an effort, grunts—surrendering words like "stop" or "no" or "please." There is too too much here. The grunts keep coming until one must stop grunting, and soon, the other, too. Fighting, fucking. The meet Grunt syntax has the grunting end in unison. Asymmetric grunting becomes "stop hitting him, he's dead!" Becomes not cumming at the same time. Uncouth.

In Grunt syntax, repetition features. Repetition can signify trauma through its compositional (re)enactment of some trauma's cognitive dynamic. Repetition can, when uninterrupted or regular, become typographic. The reader stops reading—looks for a change in the pattern of ascenders, descenders, and re-enters for new information—generally apparent as more and different letters ordered into legibility (writing).

My poem, "Big Thicket" documents a rudimentary study of Grunt syntax. In it, "krak" is onomatopoeic, taken further from language through its sensually streamlined misspelling.

to Big Thicket a**KRAK**is a buckshot   to Big Thicket**KRAK**is a
stick broke **KRAK** headlights staggering home   the road kills
buck**KRAK**to Big Thicket we go we go to sticks   to stick bucks
hot   drink drink heads light   stagger

Yet the text with which it stands in tension also repeats, breaking sentences into disarticulated units. Three men drag a fourth behind a pickup truck until their driving leaves him decapitated and missing an arm. A disarticulation. Too much.

In contrast, the poem "Well Hung" moves directly to the Grunt while maintaining the repetition and reconfiguration of the counter text.

Legibility, here, is central to a more robust exploration visually and aurally than in "Big Thicket." And though I wrote this poem before hearing Harris's harrowing Grunt, her example has retrofitted the poem in performance.

I perform the grunts live while allowing the language to play itself via a pre-recorded, then shuffled
playlist. Perhaps this is perverse in that it displaces my professional reputation as a strong reader of poems, *e.g.* the role of a poet reading within the framework of a poetry reading. Perhaps it poses questions of being articulate—precinct, it seems, of the smart NG.

This Grunt heralds vomiting. The "NG" is a grunt that in the din of signals, signals sex, but also beating, asphyxiation, and the stuttered syllable of a racist slur. Sex in this poem is foreplay for a trauma. Also perverse.

In Marsalis's recording of the railroad work song, "Berta, Berta," I imagine John Henry. How the Grunt signals his shaker, indicating the hammer is coming down. An alarm. The cold steel is heavy and can kill, driving itself into flesh, but unyielding bone, too. The work is hard and can kill. It is too much for song and too much for language. It dies to please.

Originally published in *Mess AND Mess AND.*

Douglas Kearney's collection of writing on poetics and performativity, *Mess and Mess and* (Noemi Press, 2015), was a Small Press Distribution Handpicked Selection that *Publsher's Weekly* called "an extraordinary book." His third poetry collection, *Patter* (Red Hen Press, 2014) examines miscarriage, infertility, and parenthood and was a finalist for the California Book Award in Poetry.

Cultural critic Greg Tate remarked that Kearney's second book, National Poetry Series selection, *The Black Automaton* (Fence Books, 2009), "flows from a consideration of urban speech, negro spontaneity and book learning." Fence will also publish *Buck Studies* in 2016. *Someone Took They Tongues.* (Subito Press, 2016) collects several of his opera libretti. He was the guest editor for 2015's *Best American Experimental Writing* (Wesleyan). He has received a Whiting Writer's Award, residencies/fellowships from Cave Canem, The Rauschenberg Foundation, and others.

His work has appeared in a number of journals, including *Poetry, nocturnes, Pleiades, Iowa Review, Boston Review,* and *Indiana Review*; and anthologies, including *Best American Poetry, Best American Experimental Writing, Wide Awake: Poets of Los Angeles and Beyond,* and *What I Say: Innovative Poetry by Black Poets in America.* Raised in Altadena, CA, he lives with his family in California's Santa Clarita Valley. He teaches at CalArts.

A Whole History

> In the morning they were both found dead.
>   Of cold. Of hunger. Of the toxins of a whole history.
>
>   Eavan Boland, "Quarantine," Section IV of "Marriage"

The floor is cold with the coming winter.
    I pull on white socks
and sit down before the blackout window
to think about our separation closing in.

We have a history longer than the two years
    that fitted like a shirt.
You learned a long time ago to enjoy ironing.
I always had someone ironing shirts for me.

But we go further back than birth, to furtive
    park encounters,
coded glances, tapping on bathroom walls,
ways of staying warm and white in winter.

Yesterday a young friend said it's wrong
    to expose children
to a gay wedding. The chill hit me again.
Rage spread like blood over my clean shirt.

I cannot wash it off. You are no longer willing.
    In the closet the shirt,
part reminder of love, part reminder of rage,
is held up by its shoulders on thin twisted wire.

Originally published in *PN Review*.

Jee Leong Koh is the author of four books of poems and a book of poetic essays. His latest book of poems *Steep Tea* (Carcanet) was named a Best Book of 2015 by UK's *Financial Times*, and a Finalist of the Lambda Literary Awards. His work has been translated into Japanese, Chinese, and Russian. Originally from Singapore, Jee lives in New York City.

Vanitas with Negro Boy

Bailly, 17th century, oil on canvas

I'll show you a bone made to hold on to.
A pip. A dense fire in which once
the thinking imagination sprawled
like a breathing vine. He would put the skull
on the table (*And nearest to the worn
flowers, sir, or nearer to the flute?*) turned
just so so not to be too crude. That
was the boy's job, this cage with a debt
in it (*And whose boy am I, and what is
my name?*). Black erasing blackness,
body and backdrop: you are not permitted to enter
the question light asks of his skin as if it were
a field, a mind, a word inclined to be
entered. It's true: his face, his boyhood even
(*And what is my boyhood, and where is it from?*)
would fade if not for the rope of attention
yanked glittering across that face. Look.
This is my painting, my version of the Dutch
stilleven. I'm trying to write obsession
into it, and can. Open your eyes. Don't run.
Vanitas, from the Latin, for "emptiness,"
"meaningless"—but what nothing can exist
if thought does, if the drawn likeness of a bone
still exists? Why trust the Old Masters? Old
Masters, never trust me. Listen: each day
is a Negro boy, chained, slogging out of the waves,
panting, gripping the sum of his captain, the head,
ripped off, the blood purpling down, the red
hair flossed between the knuckles, swinging it

before him like judgment, saying to the mist,
then not, then quietly only to himself, *This is what*
I'll do to you, what you dream I do, sir, if you like it.

Boy with Thorn

Unknown, 1st century BC, bronze

I.

Entered, those shadows spoke his loneliness

like a god.

2.

This was new knowledge. The kind he had little

business knowing. The mere

risk of it making it

all the more delicious.

3.

A forced-out confession. A forcing-it-in.

4.

Each push, where the blood yawned like an opiate.

Each inch, a hermeneutics of the self.

5.

Would you feed on such hurting, would you drink so much?

6.

Was he so terrible a thing to look at?

But was looked at.

7.

His face chiseled deliberate.

His face, a question gone unanswered—

8.

There could have been a thorn already inside? His tongue.
Scratching its wrongs, speaking its six troubles.

9.

How?

10.

There could have been a thorn already inside? The point in his eye.
What makes the shadows their acutest when they lift and sprawl.

11.

I keep thinking of the thorn as
marker, scrawler, what shapes the places both excused
      and forbidden
in his body's swamp.

12.

Violence thou shalt want. Violence thou shalt steal
and store inside.

13.

This Spinario, Fedele, boy with
a message, a mission; Pickaninny—
      Who would not stop for
damage, the old story goes . . .

14.

Shame, guilt, spleen, woe, shock and want.

15.

He wanted them gone, I know: all his deeper hurts,
poorer gods, that lush resentment.

16.

But failed. They were greater dark, vials of
mystery, done things.

17.

Take it. Don't you have to learn
to take it, eventually?

18.

I told him the thorn was as a key,
his body a lock.

19.

I made him meet the key up with the lock. Turn.

20.

I told him, *Ricky, turn—*

21.

He did: an anti-chrysalis, a lyric,
which is the piece of a prayer visible.

22.

Until he rewound: a new republic, a kingdom where not savagely
he was king.

23.

Who could bare the wind?

24.

Who could feel the self demanding the self?

25.

Who could see his honesty? His face more handsome
once the pain combed

through, combed like a river
too clean for love.

26.

*Violence thou shalt want. Violence thou shalt steal
and store inside.*

27.

He would devour it.

28.

This was his body, his body
finally his.

29.

He shut the thorn up in his foot, and told his foot
Walk.

Rickey Laurentiis grew up in New Orleans, Louisiana. He is the author of *Boy with Thorn* (University of Pittsburgh Press, 2015), selected by Terrance Hayes for the 2014 Cave Canem Poetry Prize, and named a best poetry book of 2015 by *Poets & Writers* magazine, *Buzzfeed, Literary Hub,* among others places. Some of his honors include a Ruth Lilly Poetry Fellowship from the Poetry Foundation, as well as fellowships from the National Endowment for the Arts and the Civitella Ranieri Foundation in Italy. He currently lives in Brooklyn, NY.

38

Here, the sentence will be respected.

I will compose each sentence with care by minding what the rules of writing dictate.

For example, all sentences will begin with capital letters.

Likewise, the history of the sentence will be honored by ending each one with appropriate punctuation such as a period or question mark, thus bringing the idea to (momentary) completion.

You may like to know, I do not consider this a "creative piece."

In other words, I do not regard this as a poem of great imagination or a work of fiction.

Also, historical events will not be dramatized for an interesting read.

Therefore, I feel most responsible to the orderly sentence; conveyor of thought.

That said, I will begin:

You may or may not have heard about the *Dakota 38*.

If this is the first time you've heard of it, you might wonder, "What is the Dakota 38?"

The Dakota 38 refers to thirty-eight Dakota men who were executed by hanging, under orders from President Abraham Lincoln.

To date, this is the largest "legal" mass execution in U.S. history.

The hanging took place on December 26th, 1862—the day after Christmas.

This was the *same week* that President Lincoln signed The Emancipation Proclamation.

In the preceding sentence, I italicize "same week" for emphasis.

There was a movie titled *Lincoln* about the presidency of Abraham Lincoln.

The signing of The Emancipation Proclamation was included in the film *Lincoln*; the hanging of the Dakota 38 was not.

In any case, you might be asking, "Why were thirty-eight Dakota men hung?"

As a side note, the past tense of hang is hung, but when referring to the capital punishment of hanging, the correct tense is hanged.

So it's possible that you're asking, "Why were thirty-eight Dakota men hanged?"

They were hanged for The Sioux Uprising.

I want to tell you about The Sioux Uprising, but I don't know where to begin.

I may jump around and details will not unfold in chronological order.

Keep in mind, I am not a historian.

So I will recount facts as best as I can, given limited resources and understanding.

Before Minnesota was a state, the Minnesota region, generally speaking, was the traditional homeland for Dakota, Anishinaabeg and Ho-Chunk people.

During the 1800s, when the U.S. expanded territory, they "purchased" land from the Dakota people as well as the other tribes.

But another way to understand that sort of "purchase" is: Dakota leaders ceded land to the U.S. Government in exchange for money and goods, but most importantly, the safety of their people.

Some say that Dakota leaders did not understand the terms they were entering, or they never would have agreed.

Even others call the entire negotiation, "trickery."

But to make whatever-it-was official and binding, the U. S. Government drew up an initial treaty.

This treaty was later replaced by another (more convenient) treaty, and then another.

I've had difficulty unraveling the terms of these treaties, given the legal speak and congressional language.

As treaties were abrogated (broken) and new treaties were drafted, one after another, the new treaties often referenced old defunct treaties and it is a muddy, switchback trail to follow.

Although I often feel lost on this trail, I know I am not alone.

However, as best as I can put the facts together, in 1851, Dakota territory was contained to a 12-mile by 150-mile long strip along the Minnesota river.

But just seven years later, in 1858, the northern portion was ceded (taken) and the southern portion was (conveniently) allotted, which reduced Dakota land to a stark 10-mile tract.

These amended and broken treaties are often referred to as The Minnesota Treaties.

The word Minnesota comes from *mni* which means water; *sota* which means turbid.

Synonyms for turbid include muddy, unclear, cloudy, confused and smoky.

Everything is in the language we use.

For example, a treaty is, essentially, a contract between two sovereign nations.

The U.S. treaties with the Dakota Nation were legal contracts that promised money.

It could be said, this money was payment for the land the Dakota ceded; for living within assigned boundaries (a reservation); and for relinquishing rights to their vast hunting territory which, in turn, made Dakota people dependent on other means to survive: money.

The previous sentence is circular, which is akin to so many aspects of history.

As you may have guessed by now, the money promised in the turbid treaties did not make it into the hands of Dakota people.

In addition, local government traders would not offer credit to "Indians" to purchase food or goods.

Without money, store credit or rights to hunt beyond their 10-mile tract of land, Dakota people began to starve.

The Dakota people were starving.

The Dakota people starved.

In the preceding sentence, the word "starved" does not need italics for emphasis.

One should read, "The Dakota people starved," as a straightforward and plainly stated fact.

As a result—and without other options but to continue to starve—Dakota people retaliated.

Dakota warriors organized, struck out and killed settlers and traders.

This revolt is called The Sioux Uprising.

Eventually, the U.S. Cavalry came to Mnisota to confront the Uprising.

Over one thousand Dakota people were sent to prison.

As already mentioned, thirty-eight Dakota men were subsequently hanged.

After the hanging, those one thousand Dakota prisoners were released.

However, as further consequence, what remained of Dakota territory in Mnisota was dissolved (stolen).

The Dakota people had no land to return to.

This means they were exiled.

Homeless, the Dakota people of Mnisota were relocated (forced) onto reservations in South Dakota and Nebraska.

Now, every year, a group called the The Dakota 38 + 2 Riders conduct a memorial horse ride from Lower Brule, South Dakota to Mankato, Mnisota.

The Memorial Riders travel 325 miles on horseback for eighteen days, sometimes through sub-zero blizzards.

They conclude their journey on December 26th, the day of the hanging.

Memorials help focus our memory on particular people or events.

Often, memorials come in the forms of plaques, statues or gravestones.

The memorial for the Dakota 38 is not an object inscribed with words, but an *act*.

Yet, I started this piece (which I do not consider a poem or work of fiction) because I was interested in writing about grasses.

So, there is one other event to include, although it's not in chronological order and we must backtrack a little.

When the Dakota people were starving, as you may remember, government traders would not extend store credit to "Indians."

One trader named Andrew Myrick is famous for his refusal to provide credit to Dakotas by saying, "If they are hungry, let them eat grass."

There are variations of Myrick's words, but they are all something to that effect.

When settlers and traders were killed during the Sioux Uprising, one of the first to be executed by the Dakota was Andrew Myrick.

When Myrick's body was found,

                         his mouth was stuffed with grass.

I am inclined to call this act by the Dakota warriors a poem.

There's irony in their poem.

There was no text.

"Real" poems do not "really" require words.

I have italicized the previous sentence to indicate inner dialogue; a revealing moment.

But, on second thought, the particular words "Let them eat grass," click the gears of the poem into place.

So, we could also say, language and word choice are crucial to the poem's work.

Things are circling back again.

Sometimes, when in a circle, if I wish to exit, I must leap.

And let the body   swing.

From the platform.

                         Out

                                        to the grasses.

Originally published in *Mud City Journal.*

Layli Long Soldier holds a BFA in creative writing from the Institute of American Indian Arts and an MFA from Bard College. She resides in Tsaile, AZ on the Navajo Nation and is an English faculty member at Diné College. She has served as a contributing editor to *Drunken Boat.* Her poems and critical work have appeared in *The American Poet, The American Reader, The Kenyon Review Online, American Indian Journal of Culture and Research, PEN America, The Brooklyn Rail, Eleven Eleven,* and *Mud City,* among others. She is a recipient of the NACF National Artist Fellowship and a Lannan Fellowship. Her first chapbook of poetry is titled, *Chromosomory* (Q Ave Press, 2010) and forthcoming manuscript is titled *WHEREAS* (Graywolf Press, 2017).

picking flowers

Grandma's rosebush
reminiscent of a Vicelord's du-rag.
the unfamiliar bloom in Mrs. Bradley's yard
banging a Gangster Disciple style blue.
the dandelions all over the park putting on
Latin King gold like the Chicano cats
over east before they turn into a puff
of smoke like all us colored boys.

picking dandelions will ruin your hands,
turn their smell into a bitter cologne.

a man carries flowers for 3 reasons:
      -he is in love
      -he is in mourning
      -he is a flower salesman

i'm on the express train passing stops
to a woman. maybe she's home.
i have a bouquet in my hand,
laid on 1 of my arms like a shotgun.
the color is brilliant, a gang war
wrapped & cut diagonal at the stems.
i am not a flower salesman.
that is the only thing i know.

Nate Marshall is from the South Side of Chicago. He is co-editor of *The BreakBeat Poets: New American Poetry in the Age of Hip-Hop*. His first book, *Wild Hundreds*, won the Agnes Lynch Starrett Prize and is forthcoming from the University of Pittsburgh Press. He serves as a Zell Postgraduate Fellow at the University of Michigan. A Cave Canem Fellow, his work has appeared in *Poetry, The New Republic*, and elsewhere. Nate won the 2014 Hurston/Wright Founding Members Award and the 2013 Gwendolyn Brooks Open Mic Award. He is a founding member of the poetry collective Dark Noise. He is also a rapper.

Eduardo Martinez-Leyva

The Simple Hour

You left to be with the horses,
high-necked but bruised as midnight.

I counted every muscle on you, at least
when dreaming. In youth you were mistaken

for a mule, body lurching away
from excellence. You could have been

the herd's head, the strongest bite
to bare the fields. I wanted more

for you. Come shape my stupidity again
as if there were feed enough

to keep you. Be like the moon,
serving her peasants the palest gold.

Originally published in *The Journal.*

Eduardo Martinez-Leyva's poems have appeared in *Assaracus, The Journal, Nepantla: A Journal for Queer Poets of Color, Best New Poets 2015,* and elsewhere. He received his MFA from Columbia University, where he was a teaching fellow. He grew up in El Paso, Texas, and currently lives in New York City. He is a CantoMundo Fellow.

Some Ideas for Existing in Public

I think you should grip your dick through your jeans and ask me

if I can handle it because you know I can, right?
I'm here for you.

                I think you should overlie me at a bus bench
and invite me to sit on your face.

I think you should track me down
the block and clarify how you'd like to split my slit open

until I pass out.

(Once, as a kid, I was balancing on a ledge
all morning thinking no one

could see me until a man walked by and captured my chin in his grip
and called me *pretty*.)

                I think you should screw me sideways right here on the sidewalk
like you said you might like to screw me

sideways before you took off
past the cop who said it's cureless to prove the crime so

come on, sure
screw me sideways, and why just sideways, why not all ways? Why not diagonal?

                I think you should whistle so loud at my fat ass
that I jump like a street rodent and you couldn't be more correct, it is a shame

my fat ass is walking away

from you because why is it walking away from you?

Why am I walking away from you? Why am I here on the sidewalk?

I'm yours.

Originally published in *The Awl.*

Lynn Melnick is author of *If I Should Say I Have Hope* (YesYes Books, 2012) and co-editor, with Brett Fletcher Lauer, of *Please Excuse This Poem: 100 New Poets for the Next Generation* (Viking, 2015). She teaches poetry at 92Y in NYC and serves on the Executive Board of VIDA: Women in Literary Arts.

UNTITLED &/OR JUST AFTER THE LAST NIGHTS ON JUPITER &/JUST OR BEFORE THE BLOOD MOON ECLIPSE &/OR…

see the same gray kitten from last week want to cry feel like a white girl almost step into the avenue mistaking the light for green can't find the Mondstehen too close to traffic at the intersection wanting to fall faux ward and fly over the hood don't worry lose consciousness lose bowel control lose fine motor skills on lithium shaking ass on top of a garage blizzard in hand think briefly about jumping think about kissing the brazen surface of the sidewalk later can't read as well eye scant focus bones feel unruly *look at this dainty goat* crying constipated food tastes like Plato plastic mistakenly birthed in a crucible swaddled in a scarf that still smells like the Atlantic that unstable house living underfoot literally in a basement caring for people's precious things all summer thought she might kill me in my sleep *i put a spell on you and now you're mine* threat to the entire world said they were attracting dark entities lineage of bastards cars out the window sounds like audience laughing when the poem is about rape

While I am walking back to Stephen's from the subway I see a gray kitten and I want to scoop it up and feed it and hold it but I can't because I still haven't found an apartment. Then I feel frustrated and dumb because I want to cry because I can't have this kitten. I'm not paying attention and almost step into oncoming traffic because I think the light is green. I can't see the moon from where I'm standing. It's a cloudy night. I feel like I'm standing too close to traffic. Sometimes I want to throw myself in front of a car. I wonder if I would lose consciousness quickly. The force of a car striking my body would probably make me shit myself. I think about how I would tremble and not be able to grasp things while I was on Lithium. Over the summer, before she betrayed me, Katy and I went to the top of a parking garage after getting Blizzards from Dairy Queen and danced to Trap Queen. It was after I was raped and I couldn't help but think of throwing myself from the top of the garage and what it would feel like to slam into the sidewalk below. While I was on Lithium it was hard to read because my eyes wouldn't focus. Sometimes it feels like my bones are vibrating inside of my skin. Nikki is showing me a picture of a goat. Being constipated makes me want to cry. When I'm depressed food doesn't taste like anything. I feel like I was born into a container where materials are subjected to high temperatures. I feel like I was born into a severe test. I feel like I was born into a body that could create something new. I wrap myself in the scarf I wore the first time I was in the ocean. It still smells like the ocean. The ocean is an unstable house. I had been unstably housed since January. I lived in a friend's basement. I housesat and catsat all summer. For a while I felt like I might wake up to the friend standing over me with a knife because she would go for days without sleeping. I will enchant and own the entire world. The same friend claimed that there were dark entities following me, infesting her house because of me. Both my parents are bastards. Falling asleep sounds warble with memories.

It is hard to feel as powerful as I know that I am.

Originally published in *Fanzine*.

Sade Murphy is a poet and artist from Houston, Texas. They are a graduate of the University of Notre Dame and current MFA candidate at the Pratt Institute in Brooklyn. They are the author of *Dream Machine* (co-im-press, 2014) and *self portrait*, a chapbook from Birds of Lace. Their work has been published in *Action, Yes!, glittermob, LIT, Spoon River Poetry Review, Sink Review,* and *Dreginald*.

WHITE BOY TIME MACHINE : INSTRUCTION MANUAL

In the beginning there was corn, a whole state
of boys, blonde as the plants surrounding them.

:::

Oh, but why am I here?
It seems important to mention all the things

that went wrong: once, my mother loved a field & fled
from the sight of its singed body.

Once, my mother kissed my father
& the corners of his lips unraveled
& a child twice his size came out.
Once, the child cried & cried & cried

until someone put something in its mouth.

:::

Near the quarry, a population of humming
boy machines—humming love songs & the National Anthem
humming drive-in movies & pick-up trucks
humming ball caps & slow dances & pebbles at your window.

:::

I guess I'm trying to explain what's happening
without leaving:

I took his hand
& the geese came back
for autumn.

I bit his lip
& the ash spat back
my grandmother's bones.

I rose from his lap

           & the dirt sunk
                       a hundred years.

I laid in his bed
           & watched everyone
                     fall into their mothers.

         :::

I went back to catch a boy who fell from a tree
& the scars folded back into my knees.

         :::
Don't ask me how.   Don't ask if I'm a ghost.

         :::

                    I know, I know it sounds strange
        climbing inside a boy & crawling
out into yesterday's light.

         :::

Somewhere somewhere
     a school of metal-clad boys.
Somewhere somewhere
     my mother is just a girl.
Somewhere somewhere
     a white man hands her a flower
& my eyes flicker blue.

Originally published in *Devil's Lake*.

Hieu Minh Nguyen is the author of *This Way to the Sugar* (Write Bloody Press, 2014). Hieu is a Kundiman fellow and a poetry editor for Muzzle Magazine. His work has also appeared or is forthcoming in the *Southern Indiana Review, Guernica, Ninth Letter, the Adroit Journal, Bat City Review, Indiana Review,* and elsewhere. His second collection of poetry is forthcoming on Coffee House Press in 2018.

DISASSEMBLER

(SIN SEMBLANZA)

I among many   in the deafening overpass
it's demolition time   the doable, forgoable self

Y LOS CALABOZOS

I occupy   this ambit, this annex
the amber of sunset   the clunkier remix

DE MIS OJOS BORROSOS

my body as is   like a bus never full
sad or sidewinding   a function of exhaust

CAVADORA DE FOSOS

through hoists and cranes   and my eyes a semblance
of premoistened ocean   no wells around

SOCAVADORA DE GNOSIS

this walled machinery   of hate to invoice
of sickness to spreadsheet   signal lights into the ozone

GRABADORA DE VOCES

no remedies to post   no theories to posit
houses unnumbered   the welt of nations

EN EL TERRENO SIEMPRE AJENO

parked in alleys   no thru-route before me
and longtime after   the swipes of empire

DEL YO Y SUS DESGLOSES

I'm too old to be carded   becoming these cordoned-off territories
mine is the skin's tether   too loose-tongued to linger

HACIENDO LAS PACES CON EL DETERIORO

in an atmosphere of harrows
on the outs of the moment

my history of landings
missed screenings

DE LA CIUDAD Y EL SIGNO

I clamber the ember
low-balls the remainder

the numbest of numbers
of touch on the flesh

CUANDO APENAS SE EXISTE

no skylights to open
when the body was born

no searchlights to warn
I for one was burning

A FUERZA DE CHISTE

foreclosing the tremors
I asked to be coursing

no view of the river
the hemisphere's causeways

AFUERA DE LO VIRAL

instead doubly stranded
I crash the contingent

as fuselage fragments
as mute and as mutinous

DE LA SUCURSAL DE LA IMAGEN

as a castaway blogger
on old motifs like

ghostwriting new entries
you know, the lyric self and stuff

ENTRE FLAGELACIONES COTIDIANAS

it's hard to buy this lyre
when it falls it makes a thud

nobody wants it when it's free
that sound is us

Y CANCIONES DESEANTES

confessional/confectional
the self's presentation

gimmicks, jimmied locks of text
in congresses and roundtables

ABRIENDO EL FRASCO QUE DICE "RENAZCO"

lugging laptops to dive bars
for where there are widgets

in search of interconnectivity
the self is legible

Y LANZÁNDOLO HACIA EL MAR

whether the analog folds　　　　　or holds all depends
on the digits appended　　　　　to the hands interlocking

DESDE EXTRAMUROS SIN CIUDADES

in theaters and beachfronts　　　where I've never been to
and will never go　　　　　　because going is finally a no-go

CAUTIVO DE LA HUIDA PROMETIDA

meaning's where I am　　　　　this litter as is
collage of bricks　　　　　　ah, the sandlots of this land

Y ES QUE CUANDO NACEN LAS NACIONES

it's hard to play these days　　　alone, besides I'm running out of days
the fires that transpired　　　did not spare these latitudes

ES DE CABEZA Y DE TERROR

and somehow the injuries　　　must become an example
a particle's teachable moment　　as if moments could do more than shimmer

COMO UN ACERTIJO ESCRITO EN EL TAJO

can the shimmer be taught,　　　shared? is there co-presence
in this promisedland of voice　　where we read with silencers-in-hand?

EN EL BRAZO MECÁNICO DE LOS PARQUES URBANOS

must we disband　　　　　　the shock troupe that called for
a new sense of urgency　　　　embedded in this loss?

QUE SE LLENARON DE AGUANIEVE Y BALAZOS

how to wear the despair　　　like an emblem we've made ours
lacking a larger scheme?　　　all I can do is lobby for your touch

Y HAY CUERPOS MARCHANDO Y MANCHANDO ACERAS

pretending the outside　　　hasn't always looked like this
and serve up this stridency　　that flows up the windpipe, this air,

Y HAY DEVOCIONES QUE SON TAMBIÉN HORAS DURAS

| my state is uncharted | and I'm ready to face the dying day |
| traders unlocking the shudder | becoming the ungovernable shadow |

O SEA QUE DESENSAMBLEMOS EL SEMBLANTE

the ether's theremin   there, I'm in

Originally published in *Hyperallergic.*

Urayoán Noel is originally from San Juan, Puerto Rico, and is the author of several books of poetry in English and Spanish, including *Buzzing Hemisphere/Rumor Hemisférico* (University of Arizona Press, 2015), a *Library Journal* Top Fall Indie Poetry selection, and *Hi-Density Politics* (BlazeVOX Books, 2010), a National Book Critics Circle Small Press Highlights selection. Other works include the critical study *In Visible Movement: Nuyorican Poetry from the Sixties to Slam* (University of Iowa Press, 2014), winner of the *LASA Latina/o Studies Section Book Award*, and *The Edgemere Letters*, a collaboration with artist Martha Clippinger. Also a translator and performer, and a former CantoMundo and Ford Foundation fellow, Noel lives in the Bronx and teaches at NYU. Learn more at urayoannoel.com and wokitokiteki.com, an improvisational poetry vlog.

99 Problems

1.   Playing *house* I was adopted
2.   or the dog
3.   I understood
4.   They made me the wild creek
between *Class Clown* & *Most Unique*
5.   The chocolate _____
6.   One afternoon the dog killed
a bird in our garage
7.   He brought it to my feet
8.   In the Bible every wing is real
9.   I could be a witch
10.   Dating
11.   Dating
12.   It is impossible to always be touching
13.   Two-hundred-fiddy to unpack this
14.   Sixty a bag to heal
15.   Inhale/heal
16.   Oppression
17.   Oppression
18.   Oppression
19.   Oppression
20.   Defense
21.   Teaching
22.   Listening
23.   Never knew him
24.   Nana packed the slow car alone
25.   Picked six honey-heads from school
26.   Drove til the sky turned
27.   a new state
28.   I don't know anything else
29.   It doesn't matter
30.   I wake up not
sure I want to
31.   I don't know how to explain
every wish is an ice cube
I swallow whole
32.   It is important for me to say I'm OK
33-35.   Fucked a white boy
36-42.   American History
43.   *Where are you from?*

44. Prozac Weight
45. Thomas and I got pulled over
    in Bed-Stuy last Saturday night
46. We were in the back of a cab
47. Taxes
48. The wilting planet
49. Sometimes I forget to take my pills
50. I do it on purpose
51. I can't feel anything
52. A clean body like a lake
      I'm some shit bodies sunk into
53. Prison Industrial Complex
54. Nonprofit Industrial Complex
55. Marriage Industrial Complex
56. Landlords
57. "Nigger"
58. OKCupid
59. White Saviors
60. Karaoke
61. Limited cocktail shrimps
62-70. *Please check all that apply: panic attacks*
    hopelessness decreased socialization guilt
    general overwhelming stress suicide attempts
71. *Are you OK?*
72. Tyler Perry
73. Hangovers
74. The western concept of Time
75. Food deserts
76. James Franco
77. OK I drank too much
78. again
79. It is impossible to always be taking a lavender bath
80. Men at intersections
81. Men in smoky formations
82. Men in the waiting room
83. Men at Popeye's
84. Men up my skirt
85. Mercury retrograde
86. My dog eats a lipstick
87. Subjectivity
88. *No*
89. *Where are you from?*
90. Lost Records
91. My real name
92. Fitting in
93. Uninterested sex

94. Teacher called me Sheila
95. Sheila was the other black girl
96. Shelia hated me
97. What we mean by "come up"
98. Be strong
99. I'm tired

Originally published in *Boston Review.*

ALL THEY WANT IS MY MONEY MY PUSSY MY BLOOD

I am free with the following conditions.

Give it up gimme gimme.

Okay so I'm Black in America right and I walk into a bar.

I drink a lot of wine and kiss a Black man on his beard.

I do whatever I want because I could die any minute.

I don't mean YOLO I mean they are hunting me.

I know my pussy is real good because they said so.

I say to my friend I am broke as a joke.

I am Starvin' Like Marvin Gaye.

I'm so hungry I could get it on.

There's far too many of me dying.

The present is not so different.

Everybody looks like everybody I worked with.

Everybody looks like everybody I've kissed.

Men champion men and animals.

Everybody thinks I'm going to die.

At the museum I tell the school group about Black art.

I tell them the word contemporary.

I have a nose ring I forget about.

I have a brother and he is also Black.

I am a little modern to the fault.

I say this painting is contemporary like you and me.

They ask me about slavery. They say Martin Luther King.

At school they learned that Black people happened.

The present is not so different.

I'm looking into their Black faces.

They do not understand that they exist.

I'm Black in America and I walk

into a bar and drink a lot of wine, kiss a white man on his beard.

There is no indictment.

I could die any minute of depression.

I just want to have sex most of the time.

I just want my student loans to disappear.

I just want to understand my savings account.

What is happening to my five dollar one cent.

I am free with the following conditions.

What is happening to my brother.

What if I do something wrong.

My blood is so hot and wet right now.

I know they want it.

I do everything right just incase.

I don't want to give away my money but here I am.

It's so stupid I have to say here I am.

They like to be on top.

I am being set up.

I am a tree and some fruits are good and some are bad.

Originally published in *LitHub*.

Morgan Parker is the author of *Other People's Comfort Keeps Me Up At Night* (Switchback Books), selected by Eileen Myles for the 2013 Gatewood Prize. Her second collection, *There Are More Beautiful things than Beyonce*, is forthcoming from Tin House Books in February 2017. Morgan received her Bachelor's in Anthropology and Creative Writing from Columbia University and her MFA in Poetry from NYU. Her work has been featured or is forthcoming  in numerous publications, as well as anthologized in *Why I Am Not A Painter* (Argos Books), *The BreakBeat Poets: New American Poetry in the Age of Hip-Hop* (Haymarket Books), and *Best American Poetry 2016*. Winner of a 2016 Pushcart Prize and a Cave Canem graduate fellow, Morgan lives with her dog Braeburn in Brooklyn, NY. She works as an editor for *Little A* and *Day One*, and moonlights as poetry editor of *The Offing*. She also teaches Creative Writing at Columbia University and co-curates the Poets With Attitude (PWA) reading series with Tommy Pico. With poet and performer Angel Nafis, she is The Other Black Girl Collective. morgan-parker.com.

A Shady Promise

> *i just want to hold you in speckled green light*
> *—Charlotte Henay*

Desire—
lived experience in an alternate dimension—
cuts through the present
here
in this geopolitical colonized and ruled
space. We have commitments
maintaining certain bourgeois and colonial
order that our touching would
shatter. Our revolutionary journeys
are tied to commitments by choice
not necessity. The path of patience and discipline
is an ethics. In a highly controlled society
how can we change it but by eating it?
If we can swallow it we can change it.
If we break it how many are broken in the process?

Whether any one of us wanted
to or not we entered
a polyamorous relationship.
What do we do next?
Name it different as masquerade?
Sometimes to face things straight on
turns us to stone.
As queer black indigenous wimmin there are things we can see
easier. If we want to bring along on our journeys
the others we love
we have to learn to
provide appropriate mirrors
at appropriate angles
so others can see glimpses
without the terrifying whole. If we swallow it
to transform it
we regurgitate bits like candy
with which others can sweeten
their mouths. Taste our futures
as shared desire.

If we touched the scream
would let loose
too much chaos at too much cost.
I have chosen witch
and have let loose
the banshees somewhere else.
Please don't
call them back

Originally published in *About Place.*

Shelagh Patterson is a poet, scholar, and activist living in
Newark, NJ.

EXCLUSIVELY ON VENUS

Roses are red / violets are transsexual / welcome to womanhood / now get to work honey

Roses are performative / violets are biological / I have very sensitive breasts / and so do your breasts

Roses are biological / you have the nicest skin / I can't stop kissing you / let's read more nondualistic queer theory

Roses are fed up / with our binary fetishes / I fucked my doctors / and stole all the medication to hide it in a cave and share it with other trans people

Roses have got me / up against the wall / kissing my neck / which is socially constructed to be a super hot strong feminist neck

Roses are violet / violets are roses / I really like you / I like you tube

Roses are born this way / violets have a lesbian streak / something about your dry sense of humor and our soft intertwined limbs / feels transcendently female

Roses are blue / violets are violet / roses are nonviolet / blue is bluenormative

Roses are from mars / violets had the whole surgery / setting up camp / exclusively on Venus

Roses have gone too far / not to be what girls are made of / I'm coming out / to my academic colleagues as a poet and I bet they will run away screaming

Roses are roses / violets are born this way / someone's got a hoard / of heteronormative transaffirmation porn you say?

Roses are cheeky / I want you to fuck me / drown violets like an accused witch / in your arms which feel like mine

Violets got a name change / roses changed a pronoun / we ate at a restaurant / and forgot to put the leftovers in the fridge

Roses are trochaic / violets have their original plumbing / let's march in a protest / then go home and we'll cook something delicious and eat it with a spork

Violets are permanent / roses are impermanent / thank you for becoming me / offering to embrace your form your fate

Flowerbeds are umbrellas / umbrellas are rubrics / I support your identification / and your disidentification

Men are from women / roses are from Jupiter / women are from men / I can't tell which is softer, your lips or this pillow or the snow descending gracefully outside

Originally published in *Brooklyn Rail* and *Poem-A-Day*.

Trace Peterson is the author of *Since I Moved In* (Chax Press) and numerous chapbooks. Editor/publisher of the Lammy award-winning press EOAGH Books, she is also co-editor with TC Tolbert of the recent anthology *Troubling the Line: Trans and Genderqueer Poetry and Poetics* (Nightboat Books). She is currently on the Board of Directors for VIDA: Women in Literary Arts and teaches a pioneering course in Transgender Poetry at Hunter College.

from *Nature Poem*

I can't write a nature poem
bc it's redundant for an NDN person
to write
a nature poem

Let's say I'm at a pizza parlor
Let's say I'm having a slice at the bar this man walks in to pick up his to-go order
Let's say his order isn't ready yet and he's chatty
Let's say I'm in Portland bc ppl don't tawlk to me in NYC
Let's say he's like, meatballs are for the baby, pizza's for the little man, Ceaser salad's for the
wife and the beer, he points to the beer and then thumbs at himself, the beer's for me.

He has one of those cracked skin summer smiles

He keeps talking like I want to hear him
Like he's so comfortable
Like everybody owes him attention

I'm a weirdo faggot

He puts his hands on the ribs of my chair asks do I want to go into he bathroom with him

Let's say it doesn't turn me on at all

Let's say I literally hate all men bc literally men are animals—

This is a kind of nature I would write a poem about.

Originally published in *90s Meg Ryan.*

Tommy "Teebs" Pico is the author of *IRL* (Birds, LLC 2016) and *Nature Poem*, forthcoming from Tin House Books in fall 2017. He was a Queer/Art/Mentors inaugural fellow, 2013 Lambda Literary fellow in poetry, and has poems in *BOMB*, *Guernica*, and *the Offing*. Originally from the Viejas Indian reservation of the Kumeyaay nation, he now lives in Brooklyn and co-curates the reading series Poets With Attitude (PWA) with Morgan Parker. @heyteebs

From I'm So Fine: A List of Famous Men & What I Had On

I never met Snoop Dogg but I met his homie Lil' ½ Dead it was a video shoot for ½ Dead that I don't think ever came out another extra assignment my sister & I were both chosen for & paid a premium on top of the non-union rate but it was not enough for what we had to go through the dozen of us girls there had no dressing room so we packed the tiny ladies' room four at a time to change into wardrobe as ½ Dead's degenerate entourage kept knocking on the door & trying to peek underneath & making lewd comments ½ Dead himself flashed cash stacks at me & got mad when I refused his proposal to kick it later all of a sudden I was a stuck-up bitch & then it was time to start the shoot we got called to set & the smoke machine was going on the faux dance floor & midway through the unremarkable song one of the goons tried to pull my sister's dress down in the front his finger actually touching her chest the AD had no control & ½ Dead who looked half-dead I mean it was like his whole aura was dirty he got on his bitch tirade again until one of the girls started grinding on him & pulling her skirt up revealing a thong & the entourage went crazy throwing dollars at her my sister & I put on our sneakers with our dresses & got our stuff & our signed vouchers because they damn sure were gonna pay us regardless because that shit was over the fucking top & we couldn't get out of there fast enough we started hearing threats

Originally published in *The Offing*.

Khadijah Queen is the author of five books, including *I'm So Fine: A List of Famous Men & What I Had On,* forthcoming in 2017 from YesYes Books. Her verse play *Non-Sequitur* won the Leslie Scalapino Award for Innovative Women Performance Writers and was staged in 2015 by The Relationship theater company in NYC. She is core faculty in poetry for the new low-residency Mile-High MFA program at Regis University.

The Whales Off Manhattan Beach Breaching in Winter

I

I have never wanted anything but to be understood and accepted,
except from my father, from whom I wanted to be appreciated,

but he did not believe in praise. If I got a 96

he thought it was thrifty to ask where the other four points went,
because acknowledging success was prideful.

I was so hungry for his praise I got to know his mind as ancient Greek sailors knew
the islands of the Aegean, how their shapes rose on the horizon, conjuring their
olive groves and the monsters in their caves.

I searched his inconsistencies for deeper hidden consistencies.
I listened for approval in the caverns of his silence
and read his eyes for signs that weren't there

from boy to man, and still he was ahead of me, withholding praise
and holding out the possibility of praise, and withholding praise again.

II

Then he got sick and very old and spent the last two years
of his life in a bed in a home that smelled like a bowel

that had been washed with minty disinfectant.
He was embarrassed by immobility and proud in his mind.

He took no visitors, and referred to himself as "The Potato In The Bed,"
and to the anti-depressant pills they gave him as "Nursing Home Not So Bad."

His legs swelled, grew purple, oozed pus, scabbed over.
He spoke like an oak tree.

His fingers were smooth flesh purses of stymied bone.
And yet, when he could no longer reach the control that made his bed rise,

he invented a string with a 3/8 inch nut tied to one end and looped over
the bed rail to help him fish it up. Patient as a prisoner planning an impossible escape,
he loved his engineering, he loved his invention; he loved his mind.

III

His weight dropped. His eyes were failing, Sundays afternoons, that autumn,
we were watching the Jets, when he said, "Shake me." I looked at him sideways.

He blinked and smiled winsomely, almost coquettishly, like a high cloud on a summer day.
"Like a baby," he said. "Shake me like a baby."

I knelt astride him on the bed and threaded my fingers under his shoulder blades.
I lifted a little, then let go. "Faster," he said, like the air
rushing out of a tire when you depress the pin in the valve.

So I went faster, maybe one pulse every two seconds, up an inch and down again. Then he
began a moan, but so low I could not hear it, only a vibration in my chest,
and the whales off Manhattan Beach breached and fell back into the water.

It was crying, but not the regular kind, because he was talking with someone
I had never known. And then he fell asleep. I got off the bed, and sat

in the chair again, and the Jets were losing, and the linoleum was thick with wax,
and I imagined the factory in Germany where they make linoleum, big steel rollers,

the smell of bitumen, and I dreamed they were slicing the linoleum into squares and putting it
into boxes; and then we both woke up, and I went home.

IV

The next week, he said, "I asked mother to shake me like a baby. She said no. Embarrassed."
Then I mounted the bed found his shoulder blades and did it again,

strange massage for the places that his heart had ceased to serve, and this time
he moaned loudly and shivered and dropped into a thick, robust, snoring sleep, as if

it was 1943 and all of the other men were off at war, and he and his friend Artie
had all of the girls to themselves, and woke up in their cars at dawn, disheveled,

dirty, thicklipped, thirsty, sure of themselves and what came next.

When he woke, he asked for water, then we watched the Jets, though he could not see much more than the field of green, and twice asked me the score.

Then, with his voice so low only a motion detector could hear him, he asked, "Why is it no one understands me but you?"

Originally published in Brooklyn Poets' Poet of the Week Feature.

Arthur Russell is a poet and attorney living in Nutley, New Jersey. He is admitted to the practice of law in New York, New Jersey and Pennsylvania. His admission to the practice of poetry is pending.

Lauren Russell

_____ than Cake

Do you ever ...

Don't you want ...

Do you experience difficulty in ...

Were you traumatized by ...

Are you sure this is not the result of ...

Why don't you have a ...

Are you on the spectrum of ...

Is this a choice or ...

How can you live without ...

            little duchess bakeshop
            petite praline sweet spot
            red velvet forest frost
            vanilla pudding muffin stud
            gilded chocolate cherry bundt

This year's fundraiser cake contest will celebrate the birth of our 5000th baby! For the first time in the event's history, MOVING PARTS will be a component of decorated cakes.

        Aunt: How are you going to get a man
        if you don't know how to cook?

        Niece: Oh, you're supposed to cook them?

The last time was two years before, when apartment-hunting in a city she would inhabit eventually. One day, after it had rained (which it does quite often, with sudden ferocity, in this new city), she left her umbrella to dry in S's hall. On the bus home, she got a text: "You left your red umbrella." Months later, after she had moved and long after it had ended, S gave her a new umbrella—bigger, stronger, and redder than the one she'd left. (By way of explanation): "I broke the other one," S said.

kitty tickler dance
catnip mouse and lunging cat
chocolate crumbs and fresh-licked pan
white wine woozy on Friday night
and damn that track!—singing
consonantal bounce

Studies fail to differentiate between choice and circumstance, though nearly a third of non-cohabitating women between the ages of eighteen and sixty

butter browning whipped puff
beaten, creamed, and almost crushed
sugar petal pinched a blush
honey, soften up your dates
toothpicks testing half-baked cakes

Chrissy and Daphne are trying out a new thigh harness. That is the entire premise. Has Chrissy's thigh fallen asleep under the sustained vigor of Daphne's grind? Daphne's mouth falls open, an exaggerated O.

cracked and yolked
that slippery trope
crusty crumble
filling's poked

The umbrella that once withstood torrents is older now and full of angles—its barbs could take an eye out if you weren't looking up.

Seriously Sexy

We are looking for 16 heterosexual couples who:
- Have been monogamous longer than six months
- Are willing to be sexually active as part of this study
- Are available for up to 14 weeks

sated, baited, or sublimated
wedge or linchpin, obfuscated

one toothbrush
one frying pan
one packed lunch
one radio blaring *Fresh Air*
one magazine on one nightstand
one stack of Christmas cards
one Frida Kahlo wall
one calendar riddled with asterisks
one cat bounding from the window ledge

alliance   allegiance   a law   a license   a limit   elicit   alone   defiance

Out (on a date?)—pumpkin soup! crème brûlée!—she looks across a table at someone's face

gooey, fruity, and bourbon boozy
hot, sauced, and dressed up juicy

The last time she left her umbrella (by way of explanation) after it had ended (which it does quite often). She left it (by way of explanation) after it had rained, with sudden ferocity, stronger than before, in this new city.

For a caramelized flavor,
substitute brown sugar.
Olive oil is more versatile
than butter—

Intimate or Intimation: which cannot
be replicated

It all comes down to chemistry
(calculation, not improvisation)

what acceptance desires
————————————— =
what desire accepts

one umbrella, a solitary red

"_____ than Cake" has several influences, including the 2011 documentary *(A)Sexual* directed by Angela Tucker. About 25 minutes in, an asexual-identified individual named Cole explains, "The idea of asexuals and cake came about because somebody posed the question 'What's better than sex?' and everybody seems to universally agree that cake is just fantastic. Jokingly, cake would be the asexual sex." In revision, I also used assorted found material, including flyers and ads, as well as Jude Schell's lesbian sex guide *Her Sweet Spot,* and the desserts chapter of Mark Bittman's *How to Cook Everything Vegetarian.*

Previously published in *EK • PHRA • SIS, The Home School.*

Lauren Russell's first full-length book, *What's Hanging on the Hush*, will be out from Ahsahta Press in 2017. She is the author of the chapbook *Dream-Clung, Gone* (Brooklyn Arts Press), and her poems have appeared in *Better, boundary 2, The Brooklyn Rail, jubilat, Ping•Pong*, and *Tarpaulin Sky*, among others. Her reviews may be found in publications including *Aster(ix)*, *The Volta*, and *Jacket2*. A Cave Canem fellow, she was the 2014-2015 Jay C. and Ruth Halls Poetry Fellow at the Wisconsin Institute for Creative Writing and was the 2016 VIDA Fellow to the Home School. She is Assistant Director of the Center for African American Poetry and Poetics at the University of Pittsburgh.

NAUBADE

sometimes you pronounce aubade: obeyed,
or sponge the face off your own skull, or let go
of a lover's hand how you amputate a septic limb.
perhaps that's too dramatic. but sometimes
he stays until the morning, spoils your toothbrush,
demands scrambled eggs. sometimes he lies
beside you in the dawn after you've wished him
gone, so you pray his breath leaves him,
that some act of grace will extinguish his god
awful noise. god bless the dark, where we all
become someone better; he grows wings
or a spine if you want them, you soften
at his touch. the sun is just another instrument
of disillusion. pray instead we live forever
in the dark, grow pale in each other's company,
bathe in the vitamin lamplight. pray we never be
woken from this reverie by a man different
from who we fell asleep beside. better to leave
before the dawn paints its awful fingers across
the room, illuminates and disfigures everything
it tames. remember romance is always a performance,
remember the song heralding the coming light
is not always safe: *i am become death:* remember
his children died in your stomach and across
this great continent you've single handedly
eaten an entire generation of young musicians.
so you sing from doorframes and its nothing
like the passion of a moth throwing itself at the blue
flame on a stovetop. no, it is guilt that compels this
song, it is a guilty singing, you sing it every time.

Originally published in *The Normal School.*

sam sax is a 2015 NEA Fellow and finalist for The Ruth Lilly Fellowship from the Poetry Foundation. He's a poetry Fellow at The Michener Center for Writers where he serves as the editor-in-chief of *Bat City Review.* He's the two time Bay Area Grand Slam Champion & author of the chapbooks, *A Guide to Undressing Your Monsters* (Button Poetry, 2014) + *sad boy / detective* (Black Lawrence Press, 2015) + *All The Rage* (Sibling Rivalry Press, 2016). His poems are forthcoming *in American Poetry Review, Boston Review, Ploughshares, Guernica, Poetry Magazine*, + other journals.

Brittney Scott

Faith in Love and Quantum Physics

In one, my brother's in the gutter,
literally, face up almost floating along

second street after a hard rain, the clouds
finally clearing, the clean stars directing

traffic, his indelibly dirty palm planted
around a forty, which, in this life,

is all he ever drank.
In another, my brother isn't wrecked.

He owns a headshop on California's forgiving coast.
He has a beard, the tattoo of his nickname

retouched to add a vine of morning glories
for his wife, Glory, who watches home movies

of when he, *we*, were kids. What's important
is that he isn't dead in all of them. String Theory

suggests there are unlimited universes
exploding every second on top of each other,

each one different, a single action reversed,
rearranged, vastly, to slightly different.

He still dies in some, in many, but so do I.
He shoots me and then himself,

and we both disperse, keep running
in so many other directions that it doesn't matter

how bad it hurts. He's just an asshole
most of the time. I've even stopped talking to him,

cut off all communication after he stole my car,
stole my wedding ring for heroin,

whatever he's done. *I have no brother,*
I say to my friends at dinner parties.

Which is a privilege given
only to those who have them to disown.
I straighten my high-collared dress,
think of him out there, somewhere,

anywhere, but where this life keeps him now.
I stare out the window at my face half-hidden,

half reflected in the glass and the shifting ring of light
left on at the end of the walk.

Originally published in *Linebreak.*

Brittney Scott's first poetry collection, *The Derelict Daughter,* won the 2015 New American Press Poetry Prize. She is also a recipient of the Joy Harjo Prize for Poetry, as well as the Dorothy Sargent Rosenberg Poetry Prize. Her poems have appeared in *Best New Poets 2014, Prairie Schooner, The New Republic, Narrative Magazine, Alaska Quarterly Review, Linebreak, Indiana Review, Poet Lore,* and elsewhere. She homesteads on seven acres in rural Virginia.

Solmaz Sharif

Perception Management
an abridged list of operations

ANTICA BABILONIA · BAGHDAD · BASTILLE · ABILENE · SUICIDE KINGS · GUN BARREL CITY · GOD HELP US (ALA ALLAH) · ARMY SANTA · CAVE DWELLERS · ROCK BOTTOM · PLYMOUTH ROCK · RAT TRAP · COWPENS · BAGHDAD IS BEAUTIFUL · BACKBREAKER · BLOCK PARTY · SWASHBUCKLE · SWARMERS · PUNISHER · BEASTMASTER · FLEA FLICKER · FIRECRACKER · LIGHTNING HAMMER · IRAQI HOME PROTECTOR · TOMBSTONE PILEDRIVER · BONE BREAKER · IRON REAPER · BELL HURRIYAH (ENJOY FREEDOM) · SPRING BREAK · ROCKETMAN · GLADIATOR · OUTLAW DESTROYER · DIRTY HARRY · GOLD DIGGER · UNFORGIVEN · RAGING BULL · THUNDERCAT · MR. ROGER'S NEIGHBORHOOD · SHADYVILLE · HICKORY VIEW · SCORPION STING · EAGLE LIBERTY · WOLFHOUND FURY · FALCON SWEEP · FALCON FREEDOM · SCALES OF JUSTICE · RAPIER THRUST · RELENTLESS HUNT · WOLF STALK · SWAMPFOX · TOMAHAWK · CRAZYHORSE THUNDER · GERONIMO STRIKE · PATRIOT STRIKE · QUICK STRIKE · RESTORING RIGHTS · CONSTITUTION HAMMER · INDUSTRIAL REVOLUTION · MONEY WORTH · RODEO · ALOHA · FOCUS · FLOODLIGHT · HARVEST LIGHT · RED LIGHT · RED BULL · PITBULL · BRUTUS · HERMES · SLEDGEHAMMER · GRIZZLY FORCED ENTRY · VACANT CITY · RIVERWALK · IRAQI HEART · RUBICON · RAMADAN ROUNDUP · GOODWILL · LITTLE MAN · ALKAMRA ALMANER (MOONLIGHT) · SALOON · STALLION RUN · LION HUNT · AL SALAM (PEACE) · JUSTICE REACH · ROCK REAPER · DEMON DIGGER · RAIDER HARVEST · IRON JUSTICE · UNITED FIST · WHITE ROCKETS · DONKEY ISLAND · BARNSTORMER · SOUK JADED (NEW MARKET) · CHURCH · CHECKMATE · KNOCKOUT · BACKPACK · SOCCER BALL · DOCTOR · THERAPIST · HELPING HAND · SCHOOL SUPPLIES · COOL SPRING · OPEN WINDOW · GLAD TIDINGS OF BENEVOLENCE

Solmaz Sharif has published poetry in the *New Republic* and *Poetry*, and has received a Rona Jaffe Foundation Writers' Award and a fellowship from the National Endowment for the Arts. She is the author of a collection of poems, *Look* (Graywolf, 2016) and is currently a Jones Lecturer at Stanford University.

Safiya Sinclair

Portrait of Eve as the Anaconda

I too am gathering the vulgarity
       of botany, the eye and its nuclei for mischief.

Of Man, redacted I came, am coming,
       fasting, starving carved

myself a selfish idol, its shell unsuitable. I, twice
       discarded, arrived thornside, and soon outgrew

his reptilian sheen. A fine specimen. Let me have it.
       Something inviolate; splayed in bird-lime,

legs an exposed anemone, against jailbait August,
       its X-ray sky. This light a Gorgon-slick, polygamous

doom. And God again calling much too late, who
       aches to stick an ache in my unmentionable.

His Primal Plant remains elusive—
       Wildfire and pathogen, blood-knot of human

fleshed there in His beard. How I am hot for it.
       Call me murderess, a glowing engine

timed to blow. Watch it go with unjealousy, shadow.
       Let me have it. This maidenhead-primeval

schemes what ovule of cruel invention;
       the Venus-trap, the menses.

And how many ways to pronounce this guilt:
       whore's nest of ague, supernova, wild stigmata.

Womb. I boast a vogue sacrosanctum. Engorging
        shored pornographies, the cells' unruly

strain, rogue empire multiplying for a thousand virile
        thousand years; my wings pinned wide

in parthenogenesis, such miraculous display.

"Portrait of Eve as the Anaconda" will appear in Cannibal by Safiya Sinclair and is used by permission of the University of Nebraska Press. Forthcoming Fall 2016.

Safiya Sinclair was born and raised in Montego Bay, Jamaica. She is the author of *Cannibal*, winner of the 2015 Prairie Schooner Book Prize in Poetry (University of Nebraska Press, 2016), and the chapbook *Catacombs* (Argos Books, 2011). She is the recipient of a 2016 Whiting Writers' Award, a Ruth Lilly and Dorothy Sargent Rosenberg Fellowship, a Provincetown Fine Arts Work Center Fellowship, the Amy Clampitt Residency Award, and won the 2015 Boston Review Annual Poetry Contest. Her poems have appeared or are forthcoming in *Poetry, The Kenyon Review, The Nation, Boston Review, Gulf Coast, The Gettysburg Review, TriQuarterly, New England Review,* and elsewhere. Sinclair received her MFA in Poetry from the University of Virginia and is a PhD candidate in literature and creative writing at the University of Southern California.

Chris Slaughter

Dear Barbershop,

Is this a barbershop? If we can't talk straight
in the barbershop, then where can we talk straight?
                                            — Eddie Cedrick

I come from you: every argument, debate and dare—
every hand-me-down bet that taught me to run

from nothing while fading the world down small enough
to doubt. No one else understands the gravity

in the way a chair turns after a fist fight, with blood staining
hair and hard wood floors. Music somehow tells the story

better than us, mirrors turn away, but I saved
the dirt and hair from under my nails. I'm not hard currency

to you—anymore. I'm no longer steady handed and perfect for slang.
You say, with every chair in the shop full "What happened to you man?

You even look at customers like they're not good enough anymore"
— but I'm made from discussion, contradiction, and cheap cognac; cussing

in every sentence just to get points across the room. I'm a glass bottle
on the ledge of some mantle that built a ship inside of itself (and the ghosts it holds).

I'm against the same grain as I've always been; believe in
the same skin fade, sharp line, and half-moon. I'm the same crazy bastard

that called the pizza man a racist, with mute Omar by my side
waving his arms— don't forget the crooked edges and what hurts,

what makes our blood agree, how women come in alone
with their boys and listen to us go on about presidents, one-night-stand sex,

and Kobe's fade-away; they listen to us throw *nigga* and *bitch* around
like they aren't even there—   I just want my name back.

Originally published in Brooklyn Poets' Poet of the Week Feature.

Chris Slaughter graduated from Medgar Evers College with a degree in English with a concentration in creative writing, and obtained an MFA in poetry from Hunter College, where he received a Shuster Award for his Master's thesis. He has also received fellowships from Cave Canem and North Country Institute for Writers of Color, and Brooklyn Poets. Born and raised in Brooklyn, he has dedicated himself to traveling and working on ways of bringing new voices to his writing. Chris is a Director of Programs at Eagle Academy for Young Men of Harlem, while chipping away at his new manuscript, *Dig*.

Carmen Giménez Smith

Rosy Complexion

Spasms, deliriums: madness is such a female world, but that's just my take.

Failing often and long at it, I do claim to know girls are there for blame.

You too can be matter, purplish and pale: the universe's chasm.

I noticed you when you got lustier by calling down a blood spell.

Cleanliness is only a necessity in hospitals, is what I teach my daughter.

She will be filthy.

I am plain. I was plain. I will be plain. I am not, though.

My bad habits are secrets, the mention of secrets, going to the last chapter first.

I do nothing with my urges because they are manufactured urges.

Originally published in *The Feminist Wire.*

Carmen Giménez Smith is the author of a memoir and four poetry collections—including *Milk and Filth*, finalist for the 2013 NBCC award in poetry. With John Chavez, she edited *Angels of the Americlypse: New Latin@ Writing* published by Counterpath Press. A CantoMundo Fellow, she teaches in the creative writing programs at New Mexico State University, while serving as the publisher of Noemi Press.

MYSELF WHEN I'M REAL

Say my body // isn't a sequin dress—

        Isn't a raw fish, being stripped of scales.

Say I'm not // a drunken disco ball

        In a lonely skating rink.

Or the deep wishing-well // the starfish fell

        Into.

Say I'm the seagull // before its bad reputation.

Say I'm the pigeon //

                But not the pigeon-shit.

Say I'm the cassette tape

Whose hair unwound // underwater—

        Whose hair // you swim through.

The record player whose vinyl

Will never scratch.

                Call me by my birth name—

                    Frida Kahlo.

                Call me by my birth name—

                    Tuira Kayapó.

Remind me // how the sky was created.

Say—

        I split the sun, like yolk

          & let the day fall into me.

If our love is a trash bag

Please // don't let it tear.

                                        You're the reason I live.
                                        You pour my coffee black.
                                        You critique the dim glow, the mint-
                                        Blue hue of television screens.
                                        You stumbled into me
                                        [Again & again]

Like a child, discovering the word
Domestic-violence.

                                        How dumb // we must have been—

                                        To hold each other so fraily.
                                        To hold anything at all—

The blue landscape of January days.
The taste of pan dulce—

The gummy smile of a teething child.
The pearl in an oysters' mouth, round

            Like //

                                        My semen on your tongue.

Originally published in *Blunderbuss Magazine.*

Christopher Soto (aka Loma) is a queer latin@ punk poet & prison abolitionist. They edit *Nepantla: A Journal Dedicated to Queer Poets of Color* with the Lambda Literary Foundation. They cofounded The Undocupoets Campaign with Javier Zamora & Marcelo Hernandez Castillo in 2015. Their first chapbook *Sad Girl Poems* available from Sibling Rivalry Press. christophersoto-poet.com.

Respect

Because her body is winter inside a cave
because someone built
fire there and forgot to put it out
because bedtime is a castle
she's building inside herself
with a moat
and portcullis
and buckets full of mist
because when you let go
the reins
horses
tumble over cliffs and turn
into moths before hitting bottom
because their hooves leave streaks of midnight
in the sky
because stuffed rabbits
are better at keeping secrets
than stopping hands
because when the world got
shoved up inside her
she held it tight like a kegel ball
and wondered
at the struggle Atlas had
carrying such a tiny thing
on his back

Originally published in *Poem-a-Day*.

Melissa Studdard is the author of the poetry collection *I Ate the Cosmos for Breakfast* and the novel *Six Weeks to Yehidah.* Her poetry, fiction, essays, reviews and articles have appeared in a wide range of publications, including *Poets & Writers, Tupelo Quarterly, Psychology Today, Pleiades,* and the Academy of American Poets' *Poem-A-Day.* melissastuddard.com.

GUATAVIT@, LA DORADA
for Montana Ray

my hair is in curlers and i'm pretending i'm so ancient i'm already dead
& backstroking through Lake Guatavita like
ALL DAY LoNG I'M CONSIDERING THE REVoLUTION & So ARE MY FRIENDS
when i hear your sob stories about how poetry is awful, how poetry is useless
i want you to get the fuck out of my way/i want you to get the fuck out of poetry's way
my inbox is full of half-finished messages apologizing for my hostility
when mi Mamá Chava, a woman who survived 3 heart attacks, busts through me
in a moment of unapologetic glory because i'm just now learning how to not care
about the efforts of the white world & how it wants to tame me
chavar is the action of annoying or bugging someone, to get on one's nerves
my fantasy is that my great-grandmother was so annoying, we called her Mamá Chava
this is a lie, she died on the fourth heart attack, before i had a chance to ask her anything
that would help my survival

i wake up on Tuesday morning making mental lists of things to ask my grandmother
i wake up on Thursday morning making lists of things to ask my other grandmother, like
how does she grow to not be afraid of her own voice

this poem's power is that it refuses order, to bug, to annoy
to not shut up, to not

ALL DAY LoNG I'M CONSIDERING THE REVoLUTION & So ARE MY FRIENDS
ALL DAY LoNG I'M CONSIDERING THE REVoLUTION & So ARE MY FRIENDS
ALL DAY LoNG I'M CONSIDERING THE REVoLUTION & So ARE MY FRIENDS
we are exhausted by academic multicultural elitism
we are exhausted by the way we must exist legibly
we are exhausted.
we are exhausted because our mothers have grown up under the feet of patriarchy
& our desire has been taken from us: we don't know who to love
and this means we have to write all the poems teaching us first how to destroy
and then how it is to love

&

ANDRoID JENNIFER TAMAYo swims Lake Guatavita–gold-plated curlers anchored to her shiny skull
a tomb, the lake opens forward like a wish: I am my most ecstatic gold self
limbs of gold
knuckles of gold
tits of gold
gold cunt
gold pubic hair

gold public lice
gold ovaries
gold uterus
one golden ventricle looping
the inside of our body shape
plugged right into the sun
lungs of gold, shimmery sacs
We are the gold throated ANDRoID JENNIFER TAMAYo
I am glorious. Made from glory
I am a gold revenge fantasy stuttered out:
La Dora/da

We wade out to the middle to meet Mamá Chava, she wants to talk about healing
she wants to adorn my gilded torso with jewels scratched from the lake floor
the mystery of the wild onion flower on her lips

and i have to turn the other cheek: Hi! I CoME HERE WILLINGLY, the language rope
tumbles out of my boca d'oro, a shrilly speech:

Hi! MY UTERUS IS MADE OF GoLD & I'M NoT THE MULE oF THE EARTH
Hi! Hi! I AM Noooo LoNGER THE BRIDGE To ANYTHING
Hi! ESTA LENGUA No TIENE PADRE

&

because I'm trying to be closer to nature
i'm on the internet searching for a history of the wild onion flower
when certain First Nations were ridiculed for batting
over what whites thought was just a flower—knowing nothing of its potency
every morning i wake up and look myself in the mirror and spit out
AMERICA IS A SETTLER COLONY FOUNDED ON GENOCIDE
and i try not to hate every teacher i had who didn't put Anzaldúa in my hands
i had read all the collected works of Montaigne before I read Audre Lorde
& the image with which i can more clearly figure the suffering of the black and brown world
is unavailable to this poem, for example:
i live in a place where children throw rocks through windows at dusk and
my instinct is to say yes, children, yes
this poem's power is that it refuses order, to bug, to annoy
to not shut up, to repeat itself

ALL DAY LoNG I'M CONSIDERING THE REVoLUTION & So ARE MY FRIENDS
ALL DAY LoNG I'M CONSIDERING THE REVoLUTION & So ARE MY FRIENDS

SOMETIMES THE LESSON FEELS LIKE: KEEP YOUR HEAD DOWN, THIS IS
HOW YOU DROWN
BUT ALL DAY LoNG I'M CONSIDERING THE REVoLUTION & So ARE MY
FRIENDS

because I'm trying to be closer to nature
i'm on the internet searching for a thing Eunsong Kim said about
artificial matriarchal spaces
these days i'm into negativity, like being less than, like being zero
like the possibility of zero to be so lacking it burns holes on all it touches

i imagine myself scorching zero, deflated, effervescent—a halo

i believe in the power of nothing
because first, fuck power
and second, could i coronate myself with a glowing nothing
i would do it forever, i am beautiful in the space of nothing in which I burn
the cavity of me outlined in pink droopy leaflets, scorched
from the inside out. don't touch me   i'm nothing.

Originally published in *Apogee.*

Jennif(f)er Tamayo is a latinx, Colombian-born essayist and poet-performer currently living and teaching in Harlem. JT is the author of *RED MISSED ACHES/RED MISTAKES/READ MISSED ACHES/READ MISTAKES* (Switchback, 2011), *POEMS ARE THE ONLY REAL BODIES* (Bloof Books, 2013) and *YOU DA ONE* (2014/15 reprint Noemi Books & Letras Latinas). Her work has been featured in *Poetry*, *Best American Experimental Poetry*, and *Angels of the Americlypse: An Anthology of New Latin@ Writing.*

GLASS WOOD

Mirror bark reflects time, sublimation
& chance. I recognize your space
even clinging with people.
I am standing under rain near the edge
of device & wish.
It's alright not running in a demon suit.
I'm going in. No shades. No blade.
I know what I was thinking—
work & levitation: warm illusion.
I have disappeared for several years.
Ask someone. My rocket is orange warmth;
may an early death do us not.
I can't guess your hunger
or match the lack of mystery of money
when I'm a stone.
Tell me to do something against habit.

Originally published in Puerto del Sol's Black Voices Series.

Terrell Jamal Terry's poems have appeared or are forthcoming in *Crab Orchard Review, Gargoyle, Green Mountains Review, Washington Square Review, West Branch,* cream city review, *Columbia Poetry Review,* and elsewhere.

excerpts from "Word Problems"

1. X is a filthy fucking slut. This can be proven by the wear in certain creases on X's clothes and on X's knees. X owns you. X is your daddy. X is going to hold you down and fill all your holes up with cum. X is spread out for you and wants you to take it. X is going to slap your face then beat your pussy up.

2. A tree branch, or a broom handle, or a baseball bat is inserted into the anus. X is not afraid. Sitting on the grandmother's porch, X knows the difference between Kleinian phantasy and daydream. If 72% of the time, this brings X to orgasm (a splitting euphoria in which X's voice becomes unrecognizable to itself), and 47% of the time this results in a delayed 36 hour period of intense suicidal ideation (down from 68% two years ago and 88% two years before that), when will X be loved?

3. As a child, X favored (in temperament, mannerism, and embodiment) the mother. As an adult, X is the spitting image (a bastardization of the phrase "spit and image") of the father. If miracle and mirror share the same root, who must X forgive? And who did X kill first?

4. X's body is covered with 8% psoriasis, 11% tattoos, 23% fat, and 62% hair. If X is a man, how much of his body is livable? If X is a woman, who covered her body with shame?

5. On Monday, X ate a banana with peanut butter for breakfast, a Cliff bar for lunch, and 4 pieces of fudge and 2 Reese's for dinner. On Tuesday, X hiked 10 miles and ate Greek yogurt with fresh fruit, cashews, an apple, a Cliff bar, and pasta. On Wednesday, X started the day with red velvet cake. If food addiction is twice as likely in women who experienced physical or sexual abuse before 18, is X a woman or a man?

6. X was a sister. X was touched by a family member. Now that X is no longer a sister, how likely is it (12%, 26%, 79%, or none of the above) that X was touched by a man?

7. There are only two kinds of bodies: living and non-living. If X notices the still-wet grass underneath the car, wants to brush it with a cheek, imagines not a place to hide but a space to be pressed (pulled?) across nature and machine. Who killed/didn't kill X?

8. This section has multiple parts.

X is building a body in the shape of a body. Silence is as dependable as conversation. Though the body's shape will no longer be southern, X's body in the shape of a body will always be from the south.

Question 1: Who is/isn't afraid of the shape of a body (aka a "shadow")?

Question 2: Who says the most – the body in the shape of a body or the hole in the shape of a mouth?

Given that X is white, X's body in the shape of a body will also be white. All the men in X's family own guns.

Question 3: What is the relationship between fear, race, and resources?

Question 4: Who is running?

Question 5: Why?

Question 6: What does it mean to "finish first?"

Question 7: When will white men's bodies feel safe at home?

X's body in the shape of a body is currently living in a car. The car is white and has traversed the country twice in three months. This is a choice. X's body in the shape of a body has masturbated at high speeds, shopped at gas stations late at night, and slept comfortably while parked on the side of the road. X doesn't understand this word – freedom – but prays it has nothing to do with camouflage.

Question 8: What is it that turns X's body in the shape of a body into a ghost?

9. A flower in the yard is 3-5 feet tall. Everything about its body is reaching – pink and purple petals shooting out of a collar of finger-like seed pods. To the north is a 48 year old Pine tree. To the west is a Black Walnut and to its south is an even older White Oak. X loves this game. The operators on the Healthcare Exchange all say "yes ma'am." X is not injured but believes certain words are a protection from injury. What are names: yes or no?

10. Everyone at the dinner table is eating. Sweet corn, chicken and dumplins, green beans, corn bread, and broccoli casserole. Family is code for memory. X's plate is empty but X doesn't remember tasting anything. Three questions: 1. How does this relate to the three black boys having an unarmed drunken fight in New York? 2. If one of the signs of a concussion is memory loss, who called the cops? 3. How to expose the secret fear of white people – what if our history kills us first?

11. Church will happen today, whether X is there or not. It could be anywhere. A body will fall down and a gathering of people will reach out their hands and begin to speak a sacred language – the untranslatable smashing of syllables with tongues. The question is not, "Who will say ni****?" Grandfather, uncle, cousin, neighbor. A girl will sign "Amazing Grace" to a congregation of hearing people. We will give the open darkness of our mouths back to her. (X is here.) No one asks God, "Which body, when it falls, will be saved?" We know what we are saying – we are not saying. What is prayer, if not the heart turned loose from the mouth?

Originally published in the *PEN Poetry Series*.

TC Tolbert often identifies as a trans and genderqueer feminist, collaborator, dancer, and poet but really s/he's just a human in love with humans doing human things. The author of *Gephyromania* (Ahsahta Press 2014) and 3 chapbooks, TC is also co-editor (along with Trace Peterson) of *Troubling the Line: Trans and Genderqueer Poetry and Poetics* (Nightboat Books 2013). S/he is Core Faculty in the low residency MFA program at OSU-Cascades and spends his summers leading  wilderness trips for Outward Bound. His favorite thing in the world is Compositional Improvisation (which is another way of saying being alive). tctolbert.com

Joanna C. Valente

I'm Writing a Poem About You in a Shitty Starbucks in Midtown

When I told you I wanted to hate
you, I wasn't lying. It's the fortieth

anniversary of someone's
marriage, the years bleeding

into each other like veins
falling apart after taking

too many selfies
& realizing I am not a red

head & you will never love
me & I will never be
Mama.

-

In Boston, a man sat for five
hours in the Worcester library,
waiting for pretty girls

to operate a new body. He asked
J why she was alone because pretty

girls should never be alone & she
was too pretty for him

to concentrate & she should take
a walk with him in the park &

all good girls are from somewhere
else & where are you from, honey,

you must be from somewhere too
beautiful to be real, he said, where

humans eat their young & stuff the bones
in a giant crate in the earth. J knows

no one really lives & this is how
she will die.

-

You took my face in yr hands
& put it on & said that I
am not a human. So I believed you

mostly because our hands
are the same size.

Sometimes, at night, I wish
for someone to break into me—

stab my body before my body
turns on itself, before the waiter

writes a ghost story on a napkin
before you become angry with

your dead & complain of hunger
on the beach—

they are still dead & they are still
your parents. There is no

gravity in you & whose heart
is on trial anyway?

Originally published in *Glittermob.*

Joanna C. Valente is a human who lives in Brooklyn, New
York. She is the author of *Sirs & Madams* (Aldrich Press,
2014), *The Gods Are Dead* (Deadly Chaps Press, 2015) &
Marys of the Sea (forthcoming 2016, ELJ Publications). She
received her MFA in writing at Sarah Lawrence College.
She is also the founder of Yes, Poetry, as well as the chief
editor for *Luna Luna Magazine.*

M4T

This guy really loves his wife, almost as much as Scott loves his dogs. This guy is straight and really hard up. This one is just that straight. This one can't believe I'm not real. This one will fuck anything, women follow him off trains. He tells me how I could have my pick of, if only, he could get it up. This guy is like fucking a tube of toothpaste. Someone should tell him the word "pee-hole" is not sexy. My mouth is full. This guy is what a diet of pizza and ranch dressing tastes like. We're friends. This one is really gay. This one is really excited to run into me on the train. This one just wants to talk about it. This one is gender fluid, so he understands. This one's got that bro pussy look in his eyes. This one looks like Rafi and just knew I was gonna come. This one can't figure out which closet he belongs in and spends all his time tying his ties. He doesn't want to talk about it. He works with special needs kids and coaches wrestling and doesn't have time for a relationship anyway. This one just knows he's not a faggot. This one sends me pics of his girlfriend sucking his dick. This one sexts filth for a month then hardly says a word. He'll hmu when he's in Brooklyn again. This one swears he won't come inside. This one opened the door, looked me in the eyes and realized he forgot to buy beer. That was the last time we saw daddy. This one is really pretty and shows me all his wigs and tits after. This one's on more T than I am. This one just wants to talk about it. This one was a 2 pump chump but I got 5. This one used to love his wife, almost as much as Scott loves his dogs but now, he doesn't. He shows me pics of her. And pics of her sucking his dick. This one's got real shitty taste in porn and tastes like a rusty cigarette. This one got my number from the roommate I used to fuck before we began our infamous race to the bottom. This one's not into beards. This one thought I would look more like a girl. This one has always been attracted to people like me. This one just wants to talk about it. This one explains what his tattoos mean. This one can't believe I've never done poppers and brings them *like an offering*. This one's fursona is a lion. This one organizes an entire gangbang that gets derailed in New Jersey Transit. This one sends me pics of his girlfriend sucking his dick. This one asks what my real name is. Tobi says lumpy-toothpaste-peehole guy is posting again. This one has experience with ftms and "is cool with it." This one is beautiful in that way that's frightening. If I saw him on the street, I'd want to hurt him or protect him. I don't know which would be worse. This one asks me to shave. This one asks me to keep my shirt on. This one won't stop texting. My last response was 3 weeks ago. This one gave me an impromptu makeover at Housing Works and convinced me to buy this red shirt that makes me look like a gay picnic table. He's bisexual but more attracted to men and he's a top but finds anal uncomfortable. He's always wanted to have kids. He's so glad to have met me. I blow him on the pier to feel like a real faggot for once. This one thought I was just a regular boy who loves cats. This one asks if he can take a pic of me sucking his dick. This one is roughly the size of a tank and drinks Smirnoff Ice. This one's hands are cold and feel, somehow, detached. This one wants to commiserate about women. He thinks my ex's transphobic until I tell him she's trans. This one's real hairy and drunk and our St. Christophers clang together unsexily. This one had his dick in one hand, a cigarette in the other and I don't remember anything after that.

Originally published in Brooklyn Poets' Poet of the Week Feature.

Grey Vild is a goddamn transsexual. A Queer Art Mentorship & Brooklyn Poets fellow, his work has been published in or is forthcoming from *Them, Fault, Elderly, Vetch,* & *Winter Tangerine.* He is currently at work on his first collection of poems, *The M4T Files.*

Tell Me Something Good

You are standing in the minefield again.
Someone who is dead now

told you it is where you will learn
to dance. Snow on your lips like a salted

cut, you leap between your deaths, black as god's
periods. Your arms cleaving little wounds

in the wind. You are something made. Then made
to survive, which means you are somebody's

son. Which means if you open your eyes, you'll be back
in that house, beneath a blanket printed with yellow sailboats.

Your mother's boyfriend, his bald head ringed with red
hair, like a planet on fire, kneeling

by your bed again. Air of whiskey & crushed
Oreos. Snow falling through the window: ash returned

from a failed fable. His spilled-ink hand
on your chest. & you keep dancing inside the minefield—

motionless. The curtains fluttering. Honeyed light
beneath the door. His breath. His wet blue face: earth

spinning in no one's orbit. & you want someone to say *Hey...Hey*
I think your dancing is gorgeous. A little waltz to die for,

darling. You want someone to say all this
is long ago. That one night, very soon, you'll pack a bag

with your favorite paperback & your mother's hundred dollars,
that the surest shelter was always the thoughts

above your head. That it's fair—it has to be—
how our hands hurt us, then give us

the world. How you can love the world
until there's nothing left to love

but yourself. Then you can stop.
Then you can walk away—back into the fog

-walled minefield, where the vein in your neck adores you
to zero. You can walk away. You can be nothing

& still breathing. Believe me.

Originally published in *Poem-A-Day*.

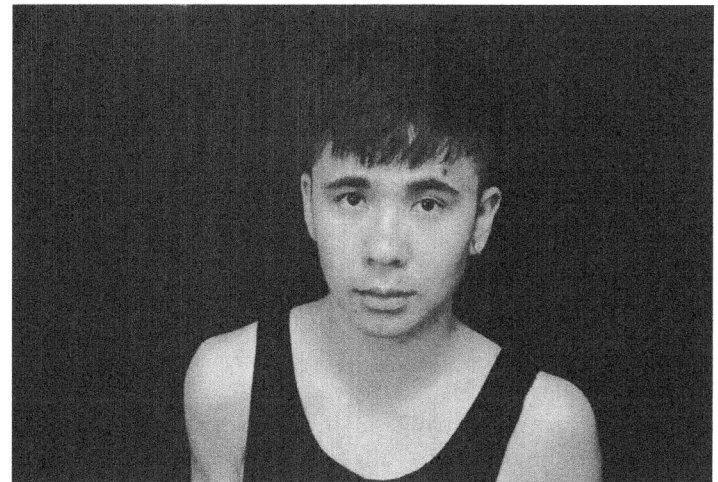

Ocean Vuong is the author of
Night Sky with Exit Wounds
(Copper Canyon Press, 2016). A
2014 Ruth Lilly fellow, he has
received honors from The
Civitella Ranieri Foundation,
The Elizabeth George
Foundation, The Academy of
American Poets, *Narrative*
magazine, and a Pushcart Prize.
His writings have been featured
in the *Kenyon Review,
GRANTA, The Nation, New
Republic, The New Yorker, The
New York Times, Poetry,* and
American Poetry Review, which awarded him the Stanley Kunitz Prize for Younger Poets.
Born in Saigon, Vietnam, he lives in New York City.

Sydnee Wagner

Stealing Fire

I inherited centuries of homelessness from my father.
On the back of tattered shawls,
I sucked the marrow
out of phantom words that pieced together
tapestries of stories too bold to be written down
in any one language
so we created a lexicon of thieves.

My father's skin cried out Diaspora,
bark from sandalwood trees
scarred from the claws and whips of pale men
who wanted a chance at something exotic.

Peeled flesh like mangoes-
sliced while unripe
foreigners don't know how to enjoy sweet things
without bringing them to ruins.

Some nights I dream of swimming.
I swim two or three oceans to get to
a home that no longer knows me.
But every face contorts to his,
singing to me muddled greetings
that my body recognizes before I could.

Shame bore me till
I tore at this language limb by limb
and suffocated it at the base of my throat,
sewing manufactured quilt pieces to my tongue,
Weighing it down with a dona nobis pacem.

Sitting under our plum tree, after dusk
there in a graveyard of pits.
He was devouring black butterflies
pulling off their paper wings till it kindled his belly
and smoke incinerated his lungs,
conjuring a fire I could steal.

Originally published in *Drunken Boat.*

Sydnee Wagner is a closet poet and a PhD student at The Graduate Center, CUNY, studying early modern English literature. Though seemingly busied by her research and writing, she still manages to find time to drink gallons of tea and seek out fragments of nature in New York City. Sydnee's poetry serves as a platform for her to explore her relationship with her mother and father, mixed race and Roma identity, and other things that take shape in the dark.

Michael Wasson

THE EXILE

> Chilocco Indian School, Oklahoma, 1922: A disciplinarian says, *There is no foolishness, do everything just so... such as keep your room clean, keep yourself clean, and no speaking of your Native language.*

For now I can
                just whisper
kál'a sáw

                        the *'óx̣ox̣ox̣*
        of your *hím' k'up'íp*

wrecked at the base
                        of a century that burns

through my slow blood

        i.

                        kiké't caught

in the blink   *silúupe*

so draw the eyelids
        shut & forget the fire
tangled among the branches

of your spine

start where the skin meets

half an autumn
        rusting the edge of winter that is

knifing   between me & *'iin*

you & *'iim 'ee*

        i.

        boy   have you forgotten us

                                is not what they are saying

or are they   asks another century

            how are we remembered
        in our choreography
of bones?

        i.

mouth your birthplace   boy
without mouthing off   *tim'néepe*   is *at the heart*

or *the heart of the monster*

                or *the grass blood-soaked*

from the fresh kill that finally isn't
                    your father

& pray *héwlekce* when your body is given away   says the orphan boy with lashes licked into his shoulders

forget *'im'íic*   because they can   tear every lip from every memory

of your mother

i.

because you are
torn & because you are
what song fills
    your throat
with the color
    of carved out tongue

peewsnúut & *hi'lakáa'awksa*
        is what is voiced in the dark
& so what does it mean
            asks the boy

i.

as the moon
glows mouth open
to the unbearable
taste of ash
blown among the stars

that the boy learned
the ghost's trail

that *milky way*
is lit by the dying

brightly echoed

   i.

c'ewc'éewnim 'ískit
so there had to be breathing

there had to be.

Originally published in *Poem-A-Day.*

Michael Wasson's poems appear or are
forthcoming in *Dialogist, Prairie Schooner,* and
Waxwing. He is Nimíipuu from the Nez Perce
Reservation in Lenore, Idaho, and currently lives
in Japan.

Phillip B. Williams

Failure of Tombs

Boy in the taut chamber of declivities.
The boy too stubborn to reveal his face.
Or too afraid of what his face reveals.
Was beauty thrown there, a field shocked
with black irises and the canvas,
the canvas not yet ready? Or the wind
had ridden away countenance? Or was light
the culprit of the boy's near-fetal curl
in the staircase where to rise and to lower occur?
Slow. Deliberate.
Light creeping through the glassed door behind.
Light through the vestibule belligerent and vacant.
Light the desire to search and see and find.
Light itself a man through the door.
Light the taking and the boy, white linen
shrouding his sex, not for modesty, not
for shame but near it, nearer the advent
of the hard of him being located by the man
in the shapelessness of light. Sometimes,
men come that way, wide as history
through the door and just as violent,
their violence hidden until someone stays
too long. Boy hidden in the slim dark,
his body learning how small
it can become like a house he remembers
after a flood took it, perpetual rain
bloating itself into a sea that takes
what stands. Or the boy is about to
stand, make of his mind a tortured capital,
Corinthian. The onslaught already-occurred.
The man slips back into the wild,
into the unseen, which is the world
blurred until the blur is what is—is all
that can ever be—true:

                                  there is a wilderness
and in it light is said to lift from rot
as though a shirt, tattered, tearing further

from a body mud preserves, heart stunned

between beats where fear had most set the pace.
Following the light is said to be like following

a self you've long forgotten until, pot-
of-gold,
the fiction inhales, the self

all bone, fanged,
its holey wings flexed to take off,
to take you with it. So

       the wind after all.

Originally published in *Boston Review*.

Phillip B. Williams is a Chicago, IL native. He is the author of the
poetry collection *Thief in the Interior* (Alice James Books).
Currently, Phillip is the Creative Writing Fellow in Poetry at
Emory University and will be a visiting professor in English at
Bennington College 2016-2017.

when angels speak of love i'm pretty sure they didn't mean

drunken hockey fans spraying fifty-seven native children
with beer, taunting with racial slurs like "Go back to the reservation"

If love is all coming and going this is coloniality starting back
at its beginning with children so young they are still learning

the meaning of words like, love and hate. And you gotta hate
the way the world works when some words scar ears so deeply

that the voice that said them still echoes in your head, still
echoes in your head still echoes in your head.

Love is action and we cannot tell where an echo ends and
Begins Let's think of it like this. Life begins with a woman

giving birth; because of this she is sacred. Yet,
our women are being taken. 1,181 reported missing and

murdered in Canada alone and the numbers in the US are still
unknown. Underreported not reported but we do have some

statistics: Nearly half of all Native American women have been
raped, stalked, or beaten. When angels speak of love I'm certain

they didn't mean this. Our women and children are being
traumatized. 1 in 3 Native women will be raped in her lifetime

& are 2.5 times more likely to experience sexual assault crimes
compared to all other races. When does this race to feel safe

and survive end? When you're missing in life and missing in
death, where do we begin? Nowadays

when angels try to speak of love my ears strain to hear
anything over the national news and media that barely,

if ever mention us and I wonder
if the silence is how we eventually disappear

Originally published in *Cutthroat Magazine.*

Tanaya Winder is a poet, writer, artist, and educator who was
raised on the Southern Ute reservation in Ignacio, CO. An
enrolled member of the Duckwater Shoshone Tribe, her
background includes Southern Ute, Pyramid Lake Paiute, Navajo,
and Black Heritages. Tanaya writes and teaches about different
expressions of love (self-love, intimate love, social love,
community love, and universal love). Tanaya has a BA in English
from Stanford University and a MFA in creative writing from the
University of New Mexico. A winner of the 2010 A Room of Her
Own Foundation's Orlando prize in poetry, her work has
appeared in numerous literary journals. Her poems from her
manuscript *Love in a Time of Blood Quantum* were produced
and performed by the Poetic Theater Productions Presents
Company in NYC. Her debut poetry collection *Words Like Love*
was published in September 2015 by West End Press.

Tanaya also serves as the Director of the University of Colorado at Boulder's Upward Bound
Program, which services 103 Native American youth from 8 states, 22 high schools, and 8
reservations across the country. She is the editor-in-chief of *As/Us: A Space for Women of the
World.* Tanaya is the creator and CEO of Dream Warriors Management, an Indigenous artist
collective. tanayawinder.com.

Dear Hairless Chelsea,

Two women are building a house
around a dying animal.
They go to the river
& dig up clay
to make into bricks
they bake in an oven.

The bricks stack up high.
Four, five deep.
The walls are thick.
They leave space for a window.
They leave space for a door.

They finish the house
& the animal says
thank you so much
but I am still dying.

Love,
Sara

Originally published in *Alien Mouth Magazine.*

Dear Hairless Tiny Teacup Pig Playing a Piano,

Your song gives me chills.
& the piano you've got sounds
just like the feeling I had riding
the train into this bright city
for the first time & so often since.
Where did you get your piano?
Because the notes all remind me
of people I know, people I knew,
& of these beautiful intersecting lines
they draw across my field of vision,
these single words that I don't
know the meanings of, but know
the feelings of, & how they move
with me when I turn my head
or walk down the street or kiss
a person other than the one
I wish I was kissing.

Hairless, it feels like you
are putting your whole hands
in my wounds.
It feels like a dream
about your family
where everyone dies.
One you can't stop having,
that strangers quote
at you on the street,
that is projected
on the wall
in your favorite
restaurant.

Pig, can we stop now?
I love your song, it's true,
I can't stop looking at it,

but I am tired of feeling for now.
Let's sleep quietly on our stomachs
& hope everything's changed
by the time we wake up.

Love always,
Sara

Originally published in *Winter Tangerine.*

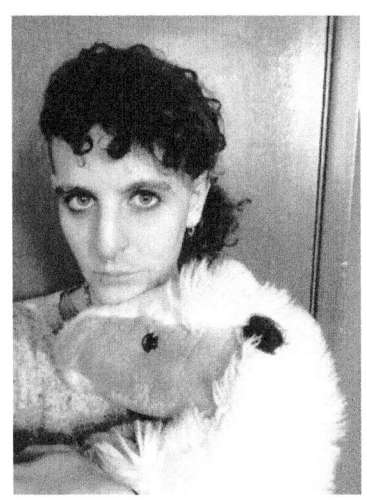

Moss Angel Witchmonstr is a human person who writes books and makes things and lives in Oregon. She is author of *Careful Mountain* (Civil Coping Mechanisms, 2016), *Sara or the Existence of Fire* (Horse Less Press, 2014), and *Wolf Doctors* (Artifice Books, 2014). She is a trans woman and a scorpio and is currently working on a novel about being a monster. moonbears.biz

Jamila Woods

coconut oil kind of woman

after sandra cisneros

ashe! she is a coconut oil kind of woman. grease

stain on the pillow, flag on the moon type

woman. pioneer of her own kinky planet. the kind

who laces her two strand twists with antennae.

resourceful, frying kale in the same fat she smooths

 her edges with. all natural, reading the labels

 on bags and shit. recycling, understands the way

 one thing can become another. alchemy,

 how the jar is filled with something like water one minute

some snow the next. she's always mindful

of the season. her curls know when it's gonna rain.

her fro is the black cloud in the water

cycle they forgot to draw in the textbook. throw away

your pantene she will, without asking.

teach you names of all the devils living in bottles

at walgreens. her smell reminds lovers

of coladas. they don't know how dry their skin is

til they touch her.

Originally published in *Winter Tangerine.*

Jamila Woods is a poet & vocalist from Chicago, IL. A member of the Dark Noise Collective, her work has been published by *Muzzle, Radius*, and Third World Press. She currently works as Associate Artistic Director of Young Chicago Authors, a nonprofit dedicated to youth literacy & self-expression. She is also the front-woman of adventure soul duo M&O at mnosoul.com.

from NOTES FOR AN OPENING

Time is really interesting in an academic sense
In a lived sense it is the most boring thing in the world
What do I observe, internalize, "move on" from, regret, jest at, forgive, invite
My family gathers in the courtyard without me
They scrutinize my usage of the language I labored to acquire
"I hate to lose" is what I say to the Bank of America fraud consultant
I wanted to craft a more outstanding mode of engagement with contemporary politics
It doesn't feel right to aestheticize received suffering
To get children to finish their dinners say "children in Asia are starving"
Is more like "at points my family has been starving"
I relate to my friend that third world factory work is not an abstraction
My family name has held the position for years

+

When the Foxconn worker commits suicide a catalogue of his poetry is released online
He describes a moon made of iron, a nail he swallows
It affects me because he is many people that I know, except they are not yet dead
He is not an abstraction
When I describe this to my friend, he is intensely interested in applying pressure to the context
of the poems' writing, how much the tragedy skews our appreciation of the craft of the poems
themselves
I am unable to see how it is not all the poem
I begin to feel trapped inside the tower of white western intellectual consideration
I feel sick, and worse, "misunderstood"

I don't want to be called the other female Chinese poet's name anymore
Or if I am mistaken for the other female Chinese poet, I want a long apology in the moment of
the recognition of the mistake
What I resent most is the punitive sensibility this is breeding inside me

+

Hunger for some immunity against desire
Which in itself is a ferocious desire replicating itself across screens
I can't yet conceive of winning the prestigious award and leaving New York
My desire is to achieve, produce, consume, succeed
My desire perhaps is to be regarded while I undertake this process over time
Facebook status is a form now, invalid depending upon who you care to ask
Fear of the loss of my white allies
Fear of my white allies

A primal selfishness leads me to record this in writing
I use the language and diction of my historically visible oppressors
I too colonize the femininity of the white open page
He loves to exist in the historical moment there beneath the red "Pepsi Cola" sign
Corporations aspiring to humanity
I lingered in the nail salon because my manicurist was also from Shandong and expressed an interest in speaking with me in my native language
Socio-linguistically it is not my native language
Considerations of: what is my "native" language
She paints my nails Daydream Pink
And the question of where and among whom do I feel most unabashedly myself
That is, where am I most contrasted with others?
An immigrant dreams of total assimilation as both fantasy and nightmare
The abstraction of my self-remembrance

+

On June 1st 1989 I was a baby carried on an airplane away from Shandong, China, the place of my birth and it was later related to me that during the flight I exhibited supernatural calm, a sense of devotion (submission) to the isolation I would later experience
I have mythologized it to the point of memory
Golf masters do this alongside prisoners of war: intense visualization over time seems to the body as good as lived experience
The imagination is, or is not, an abstraction
Three days later protestors are massacred in Tiananmen Square and the irony of the name of the place seems too cheeky, too perfect to talk about
"The Gate of Heavenly Peace"
My father participated quite fully in "brain drain"
In my adult life I throw up on public transportation
I write "false correlation," on the board and slash it red
Adults at the time say there was something in the air and mean it as fully abstract though it is fully literal
What was in the air?

+

The face of the Foxconn worker haunts me in its eerie resemblance to my father's
Suddenly laughing over the way "activism" makes us feel in the midst of disrupting civil activities, transit, the generally uninhibited movements of the public
This depresses me
Have you ever put cucumbers in your water, it tastes exactly the same
To be critical here of withholding information: on the interstate in New York City someone spoke the phrase for "Hello" to me in my native language when I could not have been further from the native location of my language
Stay with me
I am trying to dissect the moment of my erasure

He stepped down momentarily from his visible trajectory into mine and inhabited my native language with his entire being
So then, I was pushed from it?
Or I was pushed from it into a second space, not knowing here what the ideal metaphor for this space is, was I drowning or was I hanging from a high place, where for brief moments I still might have been saved

+

You open the document
You highlight what is disagreeable in red, you cut it from the page
You make no incision
You agree strongly with the content but not with the manner of its dissemination
The joke of it was how much it cost and this translation into hours labored

+

When he says "I can't live like this anymore" to what extent should we speculate about the distance between this statement and its material action
People say about others they are able to "go there" easily, the physical location of "there," quickly
I say I feel he is there and I should make all efforts to retrieve him
They say it is not an indication of meaningful potential for death
With some people by circumstance of your meeting you share a "certain something" which you must work with each subsequent interaction to undo
My friend says if men are not trying to kill us they are trying to kill themselves
What a luxury to live with such potential for action
I express my jealousy, do not confuse it with disdain
Impossible then to locate the burial site of feelings within the body
Nor am I convinced that the seductiveness of reverence for the body is productive
Nonetheless I give myself over to it
Nonetheless I see in him such "material potential"
Some words here from the speaker last night: your goals for me are oppressive
The roses outside were all pink slumped over in a bucket where I regard them and take their picture
What is recorded, how they once were, might have been

Where you cut it, it grows there double
Where you splice the tender shoot sprouts (in its exact location) a twinning of branches
This is so beautiful and non-human I don't know what to say

+

Originally published in *Literary Hub.*

Wendy Xu is the recipient of a Ruth Lilly Fellowship from the Poetry Foundation, and the winner of the 2016 Ottoline Prize for her second poetry collection *Phrasis,* to be published in 2017 by Fence Books. Her recent work has appeared in *The Best American Poetry, Boston Review, Poetry, Guernica,* and elsewhere. She lives in New York City and teaches poetry at The New School.

Lauren Yates

The Virgin Mary Considers Consent

They've found another imprint of my face on a grilled cheese sandwich.
Each scorched oil shadow a cheekbone, an eyebrow, a cloak over my hair.
This sandwich has sat on a nightstand for twelve years, a single bite
missing, no sign of mold. It sells on eBay for thirty-six thousand.

Although it is my likeness, I will never see a cent. I wonder if this was all
part of God's marketing plan. If he chose me because my face looked best
on buttered bread. They never stoned me for being unwed and pregnant.

Any marks to my face would have ruined the market for Virgin Mary-shaped
grilled cheese makers. Without me there would be no Grilled Cheesus 3000.
My face is a franchise. My face defines the words "devout cult following."

They couldn't just replace me like Aunt Vivian on the *The Fresh Prince of Bel-Air*.
That may have worked for a sitcom but not for the mother of the Son of God.

I was born without sin. People interchange "Immaculate Conception" with
"virgin birth." Really, I was born without the curse left by Adam and Eve.
A perfect vessel for Baby Jesus. If we were all born with free will, who
decided I would be righteous? What kept me from being a sinner?

Was it like *The Truman Show*? Was I an orphan adopted by a corporation
without parents to provide consent? Or was it more *Rosemary's Baby*?
A woman raped by Satan, unknowingly bearing his child. When Rosemary
said people were after her baby, no one believed her. When I said I was
pregnant when no man had touched me, no one questioned this.

The Angel of the Lord told me I would be Jesus' mother. They say
it is a blessing I was chosen, but no one asked me if I wanted this.

If I had asked for an abortion, would the clinic have burned down? If I had
thrown myself from the citadel walls, would I have survived by a miracle?
God, what if I had said no? Would you have forced me to bear my own Savior?

Originally published in *Words Dance*.

Lauren Yates is a Pushcart-nominated poet who is currently based in Philadelphia. Her writing has appeared in *Nerve*, *XOJane*, *Crab Orchard Review*, *Vinyl*, *Softblow*, and more. Lauren is a poetry editor at *Kinfolks Quarterly* and a member of The Mission Statement poetry collective. In Winter 2015, she served as Poet in Residence at the Leonard Pearlstein Gallery at Drexel University. When she is not writing poems, Lauren is working toward her M.Ed. in Counseling Psychology at Temple University. For more information, visit laurentyates.com.

Acknowledgments

Bettering American Poetry 2015 would like to thank all of the organizations, publications, and individuals who fought hard in 2015, 2016, and who continue to fight to "better" American poetry and the world at large.

We'd like to acknowledge Asian American Writers' Workshop, Cave Canem, Kundiman, Dark Noise Collective, The Home School, Institute of American Indian Arts, Brooklyn Poets, CantoMundo, Lambda Literary, Some Serious Business, Split This Rock, VIDA, Hunter College, Button Poetry, BreakBreak Poets, Mongrel Coalition Against Gringpo, *Apogee Journal, As:Us, About Place, Lana Turner Journal, Nepantla, Quaint Magazine,* Sibling Rivalry Press, Joey de Jesus, Cathy Park Hong, Joanna Klink, Layli Long Soldier, Laura Mullen, Hoa Nguyen, Ruben Quesada, Prageeta Sharma, Danez Smith, Carmen Giménez Smith, Dorothy Wong, Loma, Javier Zamora & Marcelo Hernandez and all involved with the Undocupoets Campaign, as well as the founders of and participants in #ActualAsianPoets, #BlackPoetsSpeakOut, and #WeNeedDiverseBooks.

Special thanks to every magazine and individual who nominated work, and our interns Karie Fugett, Julian Randall, and Stacey Seidl—without whom this collection could not exist.

Finally, thank you to everyone who reads, writes, promotes, and fights for a better more inclusive and diverse literary landscape and community.

Author photos have generously been provided by Jeffery Basinger, Peter Bienkowski , Sean Patrick Cain, Jess X Chen, Elisabeth Fuchsia, Rachel Eliza Griffiths, Zach Hetrick, Jonás Hidalgo, Cybele Knowles, J. Michael Martinez, Hieu Minh Nguyen, Norlan Olivio, Eric Plattner, Mamta Popat, and Arash Saedinia. Special thanks to The National Archive for additional materials.

Kenzie Allen is a descendant of the Oneida Tribe of Indians of Wisconsin. She is a graduate of the Helen Zell Writers' Program at the University of Michigan where she was the recipient of Hopwood Awards in poetry and non-fiction, and she has been awarded an Emerging Writer fellowship to Aspen Summer Words, and the Littoral Press Poetry Prize. Her work has appeared or is forthcoming in *The Iowa Review, Drunken Boat, SOFTBLOW, Apogee, Boston Review,* and elsewhere, and she is the managing editor of the *Anthropoid* collective. She lives in Norway, and on her tribe's reservation in Green Bay.

Eunsong Kim is a doctoral candidate at the University of California, San Diego. Her essays on literature, digital cultures, and art criticism have appeared and are forthcoming in: *Journal of Critical Library and Information Studies, Scapegoat, Lateral, The New Inquiry, Model View Culture, The Margins,* and in the anthologies *Poetics of Social Engagement* and *Reading Modernism with Machines.* Her poetry has or will been published in: *West Branch, Denver Quarterly, Seattle Review, Feral Feminisms, Minnesota Review, Interim,* and *Iowa Review.* She was the

recipient of a 2015 Andy Warhol Foundation Arts Writers Grant for the blog contemptorary.org and her first book of poems will be published by Noemi press in 2017.

Amy King's latest book, *The Missing Museum*, is a winner of the 2015 Tarpaulin Sky Book Prize. King joins the ranks of Ann Patchett, Eleanor Roosevelt & Rachel Carson as the recipient of the 2015 Winner of the WNBA Award (Women's National Book Association). She serves on the executive board of VIDA: Women in Literary Arts and is currently co-editing with Heidi Lynn Staples the anthology, *Big Energy Poets of the Anthropocene: When Ecopoets Think Climate Change.* She is an Associate Professor of Creative Writing at SUNY Nassau Community College.

Jason Koo, named one of the "100 Most Influential People in Brooklyn Culture" by *Brooklyn Magazine*, is the author of *America's Favorite Poem* and *Man on Extremely Small Island*, winner of the De Novo Poetry Prize and the Asian American Writers' Workshop Members' Choice Award for the best Asian American book of 2009. He is the editor of *Poems for Kobe*, a private limited edition of poems presented as a retirement gift to Kobe Bryant by the Brooklyn Nets and Brooklyn Poets, and co-editor of the forthcoming *Brooklyn Poets Anthology*. He has published his poetry and prose in the *Yale Review, Missouri Review,* and the *Village Voice*, among other places, and won fellowships for his work from the National Endowment for the Arts, Vermont Studio Center and New York State Writers Institute. An assistant teaching professor of English at Quinnipiac University, Koo is the founder and executive director of Brooklyn Poets and creator of the Bridge. He lives in Brooklyn.

Héctor Ramírez is a writer and educator living in Boulder, CO. He received his B.A. in Literary Arts from Brown University in 2012 and is currently an MFA candidate at the University of Colorado, Boulder, where he also serves as the assistant director of the CU Boulder Upward Bound program. He is an event coordinator at VIDA: Women in Literary Arts, and his work has appeared in *Apogee, Muzzle Magazine. The Café Irreal, Buffalo Almanack, Vannevar, American Book Review,* The Poetry Foundation's *Harriet* blog, and elsewhere.

Metta Sáma is author of *the year we turned dragon* (Portable Press @ Yo-Yo Labs), *le animal & other creatures* (Miel), *After "Sleeping to Dream"/After After* (Nous-Zot Press), *Nocturne Trio* (YesYes Books) & *South of Here* (New Issues Press), published under her legal name, Lydia Melvin. Her poems, fiction, and creative nonfiction essays have been published in *Heir Apparent, Valley Voices, Puerto del Sol's Black Voices Series, Literary Hub, Kweli, bluestem, Apogee, All About Skin* (edited by Jina Ortiz & Rochelle Spencer), *Please Excuse This Poem: 100 Poets for the Next Generation* (edited by Lynn Melnick & Brett Fletcher Lauer), among others. She has served as special guest editor *for Reverie, Black Camera, RedLeaf Poetry Journal, and North American Review.* Sáma is co-winner of the 2016 Robert H. Winner Memorial Award from Poetry Society of America. She serves on the advisory board of Black Radish Book and the Board of Directors at Cave Canem Foundation, Inc. She is a Fellow at Black Earth Institute and is the director of Center for Women Writers and an Assistant Professor and Director of Creative Writing at Salem College.

Vanessa Angelica Villarreal's work has appeared or is forthcoming in *The Poetry Foundation Harriet blog, The Feminist Wire, Caketrain, DIAGRAM, The Western Humanities Review, NANO Fiction, The Colorado Review Online,* and elsewhere. She is a CantoMundo Fellow and her book, *BEAST MERIDIAN,* was a finalist at Nightboat, Futurepoem, Saturnalia, and Willow Books, and is forthcoming from Noemi Press in 2017. Her hometown is Houston, Texas.

Nikki Wallschlaeger's work recently has been featured in *P-Queue, The Enemy, The Brooklyn Rail, LIT The Journal Petra, Apogee* & others. She is the author of the full-length collection *Houses* (Horseless Press 2015) as well as the graphic chapbook *I Hate Telling You How I Really Feel* from Bloof Books (2016). Her second full length collection of poetry, *Crawlspace,* is forthcoming from Bloof Books in 2017. She lives in Wisconsin.

Sarah Clark is a two-spirit Native (Nanticoke) editor, writer, and consultant. She is currently an editor with *The VIDA Review* and assistant poetry editor at *Drunken Boat,* where she has curated folios on sound art, and on global indigenous art and literature, "First Peoples, Plural." She co-edited *Apogee Journal*'s "#NoDAPL #Still Here" folio. Sarah freelances, and has worked with a number of literary and arts publications and organizations, including Sundress Press, *Best of the Net, The Paris Review,* and *Blackbird.*

Airea D Matthews is a 2015 Kresge Literary Arts Fellow. She is the Assistant Director of the Helen Zell Writers' Program at University of Michigan, Ann Arbor, where she earned her MFA. Her poems have appeared or are forthcoming in *Best American Poetry 2015, The Missouri Review, The Baffler, Callaloo, Indiana Review, WSQ, Kinfolks,* and *Muzzle.* Matthews' prose appears in *SLAB, Vinyl, Michigan Quarterly Review,* and *VIDA: Her Kind.* She is the co-executive editor of *The Offing,* a channel of the *Los Angeles Review of Books.*

Made in the USA
Coppell, TX
18 December 2019